DRINKING WITH SAINT NICK

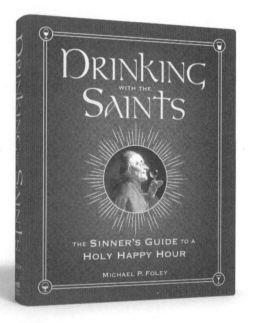

Drinking with Saint Nick

Christmas Cocktails for Sinners and Saints

Michael P. Foley

REGNERY
HISTORY

Regnery® is a registered trademark of Salem Communications Holding Corporation

Regnery History™ is a trademark of Salem Communications Holding Corporation

Cataloging-in-Publication data on file with the Library of Congress

ISBN: 978-1-62157-732-4
eBook ISBN: 978-1-62157-768-3

Library of Congress Cataloging-in-Publication Data

Published in the United States by
Regnery History, an imprint of
Regnery Publishing
A Division of Salem Media Group
300 New Jersey Ave NW
Washington, DC 20001
www.RegneryHistory.com

641.87

Manufactured in the United States of America

2018 Printing

Books are available in quantity for promotional or premium use. For information on discounts and terms, please visit our website: www. Regnery.com

To my kith and kin, living and departed—the Foleys, Rouleaus, Joe and Bobbie Forgey, and many more—who taught me the art of merriment. And to the Ryan clan, who has kept me in good practice.

Contents

How to Drink like a Saint

While researching our first book *Drinking with the Saints*, my wife, friends, and I were looking for *what* drinks we could recommend on the feast days of the liturgical year. What we did not expect to discover was a lesson in *how* to drink them. That lesson can be distilled into five key points, which we now happily share with you as the preface to our new book *Drinking with Saint Nick*. We are especially pleased to present our findings here as an antidote of sorts to the abuse of alcohol that unfortunately takes place during the secularized holiday season.

And so, to drink like a saint—that is, to enjoy alcohol the way it was meant by God to be enjoyed—one must drink…

1. With Moderation

Moderation is not only the morally responsible thing to do, it is also the more pleasant. The Epicureans of old were moderate in their appetites because of their commitment not to virtue but to maximizing their physical pleasure, for they knew that excess would rob them of the carnal goal they sought. Christians are free to profit from this insight, for God wants us to derive pleasure from His creation.

Moderation is also important because it fosters health, which is one of the reasons the Church has historically tolerated and even supported the consumption of alcohol (think of medieval religious orders and their production of beer, wine, whiskey, and liqueur). In the Middle Ages and beyond, alcohol purified contaminated water or served as a substitute for it, and it also acted as a medicine for different ailments. To this day, when Carthusian monks in the Grand Charterhouse (located high in the drafty French Alps) catch a cold, they take a tablespoon of their delicious herbal liqueur, chartreuse.

Lastly, moderation is key to fostering fellowship. Drinking just enough to relax the tongue but not enough to have it reel away from dispassionate thought is highly conducive to good conversation and camaraderie. As the poet Ogden Nash puts it in his poem "Reflections on an Ice Breaker," "Candy is dandy but liquor is quicker."

2. With Gratitude

Moderation is also an expression of gratitude to God for the goodness of the grape and the grain. As Chesterton puts it: "We should thank God for beer and burgundy by not drinking too much of them." Gratitude is a much-ignored virtue these days, as we fixate more and more on our rights and entitlements and less on what we owe to others. Indeed, for some modern philosophers such as Kant, gratitude is a bad thing, a threat to our autonomy, for it implies that we are in someone else's debt.

But for the Christian, it is a joy to give thanks to the God who creates, redeems, and sanctifies us and to see His goodness in all the goods around us, including those in our glass. Such gratitude should be especially prominent during the Christmas season, which recalls the astonishing fact that God freely chose to humiliate Himself by taking on lowly human flesh and being born in a stinky stable, all out of His delirious love for us. All genuine Christian culture, including the cultivation and consumption of strong drink, is a grateful response to God's love. Note the gratitude fermenting in this statement by St. Arnold of Metz, a patron saint of brewers: "From man's sweat and God's love, beer came into the world."

3. With Memory

Catholic piety is centered on the Eucharist, which means "thanksgiving," and hence an attitude of gratitude permeates all aspects of Catholic life. But the Eucharist is also a memorial, a fulfillment of the command to "Do this in memory of Me." Gratitude requires memory, specifically, the memory of the good things undeservedly given to us.

One of the key differences between healthy and unhealthy drinking is whether the imbiber is drinking to remember or drinking to forget. Consider the difference between the drinking that goes on at a truly good and noble wedding and the drinking that often goes on at a bar. At a good wedding, multiple generations gather to celebrate the triumphant and honorable nuptials of a faithful man and a faithful woman; they gather to celebrate the love of this new couple which, God willing, will only grow over the years and lead to more children and more love. And when they do so, they also remember the love in their own marriages, the love in their parents' marriages, and on and on. They remember a great chain of love, and they raise their glasses to it. And something similar obtains at a great Christmas festivity, when loved ones from several generations gather to celebrate and remember the love of the Christ Child.

Contrast this picture with that of a solitary man at the end of the bar drinking alone. He laments his loneliness, his dead-end job, his lost youth. The man orders round after round not to remember the good but to forget the bad. Such a use of the drink falls far from the fine art of Christian quaffing.

4. With Merriment

Another way to consider the difference between healthy and unhealthy drinking is to reflect on the notions of "fun" and "merriment." "Fun" implies a form of entertainment that is not necessarily bad but is usually superficial and can be enjoyed alone. Perhaps a young man would have more fun playing video games with his friends, but it is conceivable that he can still have some fun playing the game by himself.

"Merriment," on the other hand, necessitates fellowship. People usually do not make merry alone in a room; they make merry at a festival or a great banquet—hence the phrase, "the more the merrier." At least to our mind, merriment presupposes strong community and a truly divine and memorable reason to celebrate: think of how absurd it would be to say "Merry Administrative Professionals' Day." But "Merry Christmas" still has real theological meaning, and not just because Christ's Mass is mentioned. When we wish someone to be merry on Our Lord's birthday, aren't we hoping that he or she will have more than just a good time? Aren't we invoking a kind of blessing upon them? There is almost something sacred about real merriment.

Of course, all of this involves risk: there is an obsolete term in English, "merry-drunk," that suggests as much. But as Josef Pieper points out in his work *In Tune with the World: A Theory of Festivity*, all festivity contains "a natural peril and a germ of degeneration" because all festivity carries with it an element of lavishness. But just as lavishness need not involve decadence, "wet" merriment need not involve drowning.

5. With Ritual

Pieper's book calls to mind another aspect of merriment: ritual. "The ritual festival," Pieper goes so far as to assert, "is the most festive form of festivity." How? Because true festive joy cannot exist without God and without a tradition of celebration involving ritual praise and sacrifice. Without religious ritual, Pieper concludes, a holiday becomes not a "profane festival" but something worse: a contrived and artificial occasion that becomes a "new and more strenuous kind of work."

We pious drinkers can appropriate Pieper's wisdom with two simple practices. First, our celebrations should be grounded in the liturgical year, that grand recurring narrative of the mysteries of Christ and His saints. Catholic liturgy, Pieper writes, "is in fact 'an unbounded Yea-and Amen-saying' to the "whole of reality and existence," and each saint's feast day is both a celebration of a saint's having said Yes to God and an invitation for us to do so as well. And, of course, this celebration takes on added meaning during the Advent and Christmas seasons, when we ritually anticipate and rejoice in the Word made flesh at the same time that we honor those saints whose feast days flank, as it were, the Lord's manger.

Second, there should be some ritual component to one's celebration, no matter how humble. The easiest way to accomplish this goal is with the ritual of a toast. In *Drinking with Saint Nick*, the last part of an entry is often a call-out entitled "Last Call" that features a toast. Toasting is about as old as drinking itself and has deeply religious roots. The original "libation," along with uttering some invocation to the divine, consisted of pouring out the first portion of one's drink to the gods. And according to one account, the custom of clinking glasses is a Christian invention, its tinkling sound imitating the peal of church bells driving away demons. Catholics should be natural toasters, for ritual is in our blood: we recognize that formality does not replace spontaneity or joy but completes it, channels it, enriches it. And the universal desire to toast to someone's health finds new meaning in the high Christian aspiration for more than a mere absence of bodily ills. All it takes is one toast to make your amorphous get-together an event, perhaps even a holy one.

May the joys of this sacred season gladden your hearts now and throughout the year. Wassail!

> —**Mike and Alexandra Foley** and their merry
> band of Drinkers with the Saints
>
> Advent "Stir Up" Sunday 2017

How to Use This Book

In May 2015, we published *Drinking with the Saints: The Sinner's Guide to a Holy Happy Hour* (Regnery), in which we paired beer, wine, and cocktail suggestions with the feast days of the Church year. The book was an instant success, and soon there were calls for more rounds. Like a good host, we are only too happy to oblige. Just in time for the holidays, we are pleased to present *Drinking with Saint Nick*, a book that draws from the original but presents new material never seen before. In *Drinking with Saint Nick* you will find:

- Drinks for every day in December leading up to Christmas: a "wet" Advent Calendar, if you will
- Drinks for "The Golden Nights" (December 17-23), a special period of preparation before Christmas
- Drinks for the Twelve Days of Christmas, which begin on December 25 and end on January 5

- Drinks for each verse of the Christmas carol "The Twelve Days of Christmas"
- Drinks for the Feast of Epiphany (January 6) and a few straggler feasts thereafter

With *Drinking with Saint Nick* in your possession, your holiday drinking and party needs are more than covered.

FORMATTING, FLIPPING, AND PLANNING

There are sixty-three entries in this book: forty-four calendar days and two overlapping sections: The Golden Nights and the "Twelve Days of Christmas" song. When preparing for a soiree, feel free to toggle back and forth until you find something you like. Aren't crazy about the drinks for Our Lady of Solitude on December 18? Then see what the offerings are on the second Golden Night. Not interested in the recommendations for Childermas on December 28? Then check out the fourth day of the "Twelve Days" song with its theme of Four Calling Birds. In fact, do not limit yourself to the calendar but feel free to combine suggestions from any part of the book to slake your guests' thirst. For the letter killeth, but the spirit quickeneth.

Recipes are in separate call-out boxes, but be sure to consult the main text as well for other drink suggestions. And don't forget the "Last Call" feature, which provides toasts and other ideas for your festivity.

Regarding the entries for calendar days: there will occasionally be two dates, one immediately following the title and one in parentheses. The first date is that of the traditional Roman calendar in use until 1969, the second that of the post-Vatican II calendar. Often, however, the two calendars are the same, in which case only one date is shown.

As for planning, apply the Boy Scout rule of being prepared to the Adult Swim of your happy hour. You would have to be a serious sot to already own every ingredient mentioned in this book, so be sure to shop ahead for what you don't have. Perhaps you and your beloved can give each other one or two bottles for Christmas that are currently not in your liquor cabinet—it will be a happy confirmation of the cliché that it is better to give than to receive. Another suggestion is to see if your liquor store has a desired but seldom-to-be-used item in a small bottle, such as 50 ml or 375 ml (these are generally found on or behind the cashier's counter). And if they don't have the item at all, see if they can order it for you. Liquor chains often have merchandise at one branch but not another because of variations in local taste, but they can ship a product to the branch near you. Failing that, you can always make a "packy run" (as they say in New England) the next time you visit a more cosmopolitan center. Finally, you can find some items such as bitters and syrups online.

A Note on Our Selection Process

Our beer and wine suggestions speak for themselves: the only thing we cannot predict is their availability in your locale, which will vary greatly according to state and county laws and market forces. We figured that with beer and wine it would be better to cast the net wide by mentioning as many as we could, including limited regional offerings, rather than have you miss out on a good microbrew or vintage that may be in your neck of the woods.

The availability of liquors and liqueurs also varies greatly from place to place, but here we followed a somewhat different logic. It may not always seem like it, but we tried not to include too many cocktail recipes that require rare or unusual ingredients—no easy feat in this age of ever more creative libations. With only a few exceptions, we used our adopted hometown of Waco, Texas as the canary in the mine. Waco's alcohol retail market is not as vast as that of a major metropolis, but neither is it a dry town. We reckoned that if we could find an ingredient in our area, chances are good that you can too. And it is for you, and not the high-falutin' mixologists living in the big city, that we are writing this book.

As for how we paired specific drink suggestions with this or that feast day, we let the Spirit be our guide to the spirits, allowing a variety of associations, no matter how tangential, to inform our decisions. In endorsing our flagship *Drinking with the Saints*, Fr. Mitch Pacwa playfully remarked that the book's connections "between the saints and [its] featured beverages may be as strained as some of the cocktails, but they are just as interesting." Our only objection to this observation is: *may* be strained? Let us be clear. It is not true that parts of *Drinking with the Saints* and now *Drinking with Saint Nick* are a stretch; rather, their *entire content* is a stretch. We are, after all, creating a dubious new genre: the Catholic cocktail manual.

CRISIS OF FAITH

In *Drinking with the Saints*, we offered a variety of tips for hosting a pious party. Our recommendations still stand, with two exceptions. Since the publication of our first book, we have had a crisis of faith, and we need to confess it before you and Our Lord. It is this: we have changed our opinion on the infamous shaking versus stirred controversy. We initially privileged shaking all cocktails because of the cool look that the little shards of ice have as they float on the surface of the drink. But shaking, we have since come to learn, is not always the right call. Depending on the ice used, shaking tends to water down a drink more than stirring, thus diluting its taste. We have all heard from James Bond that a martini should be shaken not stirred, but 007 made that call in the 1950s, when the proof of liquor was generally higher than it is today. It therefore made sense back then to go with shaking, which is why all the bartenders' books from the 1920s on recommended it.

Bond also preferred a vodka martini, and vodka, especially when made from potatoes, is oilier than gin; shaking was said to disperse the oil better. But a gin martini is another matter. Gin, it is said, "bruises" when shaken; and like an insecure person with a fragile ego, when gin is bruised, it grows bitter. Hence a stirred gin martini is smoother than its shaken counterpart, with less of a sharp aftertaste.

As good Catholics, we were understandably confused about these new doctrines (new to us anyway), and since the pope and the Magisterium refused to answer our *dubia*, we decided to do a blind taste test. To our surprise, we found that we preferred the stirred martini over the shaken. Since we don't want to force our religion on you, we suggest that you try the same experiment yourself. We can at least assure you that, in this case at least, the new policy is not inconsistent with immemorial teaching.

So now our rule of faith is this: When any of the ingredients are opaque—such as citrus juices, dairy, or eggs—shaking is the best way to mix those ingredients up. But for clear ingredients, go with stirring. Stirring does, however, take longer than shaking to chill a drink, so be prepared to put a little more effort into the preparation. In *Drinking with Saint Nick*, we recommend stirring

forty times just as we recommend shaking forty times—
it is the biblical number for penance and a good mortifi-
cation prior to your reward. And those cool bar spoons
with the spiral handles make it easy to stir and spin the
spoon at the same time for maximum effect.

In *Drinking with Saint Nick* we generally preserve the
original recipe, including the inventor's instructions on
shaking or stirring, but let your conscience and your
patience be your guide.

A Cherry Jubilee

Second, we have come to learn that not all cherries are
created equal. Most cocktail recipes call for a generic maraschino cherry, but if you want the gold standard in these
little red babies, then look no further than the rich taste of
Luxardo's Original Maraschino Cherries. Luxardo, however, can be pricey, so our daily driver for cherries is now
Toschi's amarena black cherries—in our opinion, the best
value overall. (Our local supermarket has them, but you
can often get a better deal by buying in larger quantities on
amazon.com.) We're not trying to turn you into snobs, but
once you try Luxardo or Toschi, the cheap maraschino
cherries will taste like soggy balls of wax.

The Parting Glass

Despite some changes in our taste, our goal nevertheless
remains the same: to encourage Catholic friendship and

merriment and to increase the number of pious festivities across the land. For us, drinking is not so much about drinking as it is about fellowship, and that is especially true during the Christmas holidays, hailed from the first moments of English Christendom as the time of good cheer and "wassail" (see p. 110). It is our hope that *Drinking with Saint Nick* will help wash out the bad aftertaste left by consumerism, raucous office parties, or the holiday rush, and enable you and yours to recover the original joy, innocence, and cheer of waiting for, celebrating, and raising a glass to the Christ Child. Wassail!

ADVENT CALENDAR
FROM DECEMBER 1–24

You may have seen those Advent Calendars with little bottles of whiskey for each of the first twenty-four days of December. We like the idea, but the portions can be awfully small and the variety sometimes wanting. A better alternative, we think, is an Advent Calendar of cocktail, beer, and wine suggestions with the saints' days as our inspiration.

But really: drinking during Advent? Although Americans have long abandoned the penitential aspects of the weeks before Christmas for shopping sprees and bacchanalian holiday shindigs, there are still a number of pious folks who want to keep a tight rein on merry-making until the actual feast of Christmas. So do we, but keeping your powder dry for the Twelve Days of Christmas does not mean that you can't get in a little target practice beforehand. And it may be the case that the only opportunity you will have to make merry with friends is during Advent, before they leave town for a long Christmas vacation.

But before we present the *Drinking with Saint Nick* Wet Advent Calendar, here are some generic suggestions for Advent as well as some specific suggestions for a couple of its Sundays.

THE DAYS OF ADVENT

An excellent option to warm the frosty nights of Advent is German mulled wine. Known as "glow wine" because of the hot irons once used to make it, Glühwein or Glüwein is traditionally consumed during the winter around Christmas, although it is also associated with the season of Advent. Here is a simple recipe for one person, followed by another for two to four.

GLÜHWEIN (INDIVIDUAL)

4 oz. claret (or any hearty, dry red wine)
1 stick cinnamon
½ tsp. sugar

1 orange peel
1 lemon peel
1 whole clove

Build in a small saucepan, bring to the boiling point, let cool a little, and serve in Irish coffee cups or coffee mugs. (Note: do not allow the mix to boil, or the alcohol will evaporate—unless, of course, you are serving children and want it to evaporate.)

GLÜHWEIN (SERVES 2-4)

1 bottle of claret or any hearty, dry red wine
3 sticks cinnamon
3 tbsp. sugar

1 orange, sliced
1 lemon, sliced
3 whole cloves
cardamom or ginger, to taste

Build in a saucepan, bring to the boiling point, let cool a little, and serve in Irish coffee cups or coffee mugs. (Note: do not allow the mix to boil, or the alcohol will evaporate—unless, of course, you are serving children and want it to evaporate.)

ADVENT SUNDAY OR FIRST SUNDAY OF ADVENT

The beginning of the liturgical year is also called Stir-Up Sunday because the Collect in the traditional Missal begins with the words, "Stir up, we beseech Thee." Stir-Up Sunday also became the occasion for stirring up Christmas pudding in preparation for the great holiday. It even inspired a little ditty:

> Stir up, we beseech Thee,
> The pudding in the pot;
> And when we get home
> We'll eat the lot.

As we mentioned in the introduction, cocktails with clear ingredients are better stirred while cocktails with opaque ingredients such as lime juice are better shaken (pp. xxii). In honor of Stir Up Sunday, guess which kind you should focus on tonight.

With one exception: If you are following the 1962 Missal or if the readings in the new Missal have as the Gospel this year the ominous Matthew 24:36-44, toast to the end of the world with the magnificent cocktail called the Last Word (which must be shaken).

LAST WORD

¾ oz. gin   ¾ oz. maraschino liqueur
¾ oz. green chartreuse   ¾ oz. lime juice

Pour all ingredients into a shaker filled with ice and shake
forty times. Strain into a cocktail glass.

GAUDETE SUNDAY, OR
THIRD SUNDAY OF ADVENT

Most folks remember this Sunday in Advent as the one
where the priest wears "pink" vestments. Just don't say
that to the priest or he'll never wear them again (priests
are men too, after all). The technical name for this
beautiful liturgical hue is rose. Symbolically, rose can
be seen as a lighter shade of the penitential color of
violet, and thus it still evokes the penitence of the season but with an added dimension of joyful anticipation. The name Gaudete or "Rejoice" comes from the
opening word of the traditional Introit (Entrance Antiphon) and the theme of the Epistle; it expresses the
jubilance of waiting with hopeful certainty in the
Lord's fulfillment of His promises. The Sunday also
constitutes a slight relaxation of the rigors of Advent,
a sort of catching of one's breath before the final penitential push.

And *Drinking with Saint Nick* is all about exploiting such relaxations. Catch your breath tonight with

a pink or rose-colored cocktail. Have recourse to your favorite one, or try one of the three we recommend here. Let's start with the classic Pink Gin, made famous by Great Britain's Royal Navy in the nineteenth century. In 1824 it was discovered that bitters could cure seasickness. To encourage sailors to drink them, the Navy served bitters with something it knew its seamen would like—gin. To be more specific, the High Command mixed bitters, which gives the drink its pink color, with "sweet" Plymouth gin instead of "dry" London gin.

PINK GIN

1½ oz. Plymouth gin, chilled   **1 lemon twist**
1 dash Angostura bitters

Take a chilled cocktail glass, add the bitters, and coat the interior of the glass with the bitters by swirling it around. Add gin and garnish with lemon twist.

You can also dazzle your friends with your knowledge by asking them if you "want it in or out", that is, if they want the remaining bitters tossed out after it has coated the glass or left in.

If you have only dry London gin on hand, try a Pink Rose.

PINK ROSE

1½ oz. gin
¼ oz. grenadine
¼ oz. cream

1 egg white
¼ oz. lemon juice

Pour all ingredients into a shaker filled with ice and shake forty times. Strain into a cocktail glass.

Or, try this lovely and refreshing libation that we discovered in a 1934 cocktail manual. It is called a Bacardi Cocktail, but in our household we refer to it as a Jubilee.

BACARDI COCKTAIL

2 oz. Bacardi rum
½ oz. grenadine

½ oz. lemon juice

Pour all ingredients into a shaker filled with ice and shake forty times. Strain into a cocktail glass.

ST. EDMUND CAMPION, DECEMBER 1

Edmund Campion (1540–1581) was a rising star in Elizabethan England and in the Anglican Church when he threw it all away for union with the Bishop of Rome. Campion first fled to Ireland, where he escaped arrest and torture by adopting the pseudonym "Mister

Patrick." He then studied at the Catholic English College of Douai in France and, after being ordained a priest in the Society of Jesus, taught rhetoric and philosophy at the Jesuit college in Prague. In 1580, when the Jesuits began a mission to England, St. Edmund was among them. The night before he left, one of his fellow priests was moved to write over his doorway: "Father Edmund Campion, Martyr."

Word that the famous Edmund Campion was return-

ing to England caused a sensation, even though he was traveling incognito as a jewel merchant. Campion was eventually betrayed, arrested, and tortured. During his trial, he conducted himself so well (despite having no means of preparing a defense) that some in the courtroom found themselves hoping for his acquittal. But Campion was found guilty anyway and condemned to be hanged, drawn, and quartered; he not only forgave the man who betrayed him but helped to save his life.

Campion was no shrinking violet. After he and several other Catholics were condemned, he told the jury: "In condemning us, you condemn all your own ancestors, all our ancient bishops and kings, all that was once the glory of England—the island of saints, and the most devoted child of the See of Peter."

Colleen Graham, inventor of the following version of the Hot Gin Toddy, recommends a traditional London dry gin such as Tanqueray because of its distinctive juniper-forward profile that opens up in botanical splendor when mixed with hot water. Hot water is what St. Edmund found himself in for keeping to the ancient traditions of England after he was bitterly betrayed (the toddy's lemon juice) and given the sweet crown of martyrdom (the sugar). Finally, the cinnamon stick can be said to represent the knife in the saint's chest, a common symbol for him in Christian art.

HOT GIN TODDY

By Colleen Graham

1 teaspoon sugar

2 oz. hot water

1½ oz. Tanqueray London Dry Gin

cinnamon stick for garnish

¾ oz. lemon juice

Build sugar and hot water in a heat-resistant brandy snifter or Irish coffee mug and stir until the sugar is dissolved. Add gin and lemon juice and stir. Garnish with cinnamon stick.

LAST CALL

The great novelist Evelyn Waugh wrote a magnificent biography of our saint entitled *Edmund Campion: A Life* (1935). It is worth cracking open with a Hot Gin Toddy on a cold winter's night. Or if you will be drinking with companions tonight, you can turn Campion's words to the jury into a toast. "To St. Edmund Campion, priest and martyr: may his prayers and example help us honor our ancestors, our ancient bishops and kings, and all that was once the glory of Christendom."

ST. BIBIANA, DECEMBER 2

Just when it looked like the Church would no longer suffer persecution from the Romans thanks to Constantine's Edict of Toleration, Julian the Apostate became emperor and renewed government hostilities (hell hath no fury like an ex-Catholic). One of the victims of Julian's policies was St. Bibiana (d. 363), a Christian noblewoman who was scourged to death for her faith. Bibiana's home became a church on the Aventine Hill in Rome; in the nearby garden grew an herb reputed to cure headaches and epilepsy. Consequently, St. Bibiana became the patron saint of headaches, epilepsy, and hangovers.

A Bloody Mary (see p. 133) would be a fitting potation for today's saint, since it too is believed to have curative properties from the previous night's overindulgence. And the Bloody Mary, which is served in a highball glass and has a reddish hue, has the added advantage of resembling the coral-colored column to which St. Bibiana was bound during her scourging and which is currently venerated as a relic in her church.

WINE

In honor of St. Bibiana's home/church on the Aventine, have a bottle of Australia's Sevenhill Cellars, named by the Jesuits after the seven hills of Rome.

LAST CALL

To the patroness of hangovers we pray: Through the intercession of St. Bibiana, may we never need the intercession of St. Bibiana.

ST. FRANCIS XAVIER, DECEMBER 3

The Spanish-born St. Francis Xavier (1506–1552) became one of the first seven founding Jesuits when he was won over by his classmate, St. Ignatius of Loyola, in Paris. Francis was sent to India, where he is said to have converted more people to the Faith than any other

person in history except the Apostle St. Paul. St. Francis Xavier also conducted missions in Indonesia and Japan and died at the age of forty-six as he was trying to enter into China, his great dream as a missionary.

It's unlikely that the Francis Cocktail was named after St. Francis Xavier, but it contains some of our favorite ingredients, which in turn can symbolize aspects of the saint's life: brandy for his Spanish ancestry, dry or French vermouth for his education in Paris, Grand Marnier ("great mariner") for his missionary travels overseas, and Beefeater gin for his work in India. Beefeater is made in England and is named after the Yeoman Warders at the Tower of London, but the Beefeater was a global icon for "Britishness" that no doubt rubbed the Hindu Indians, for whom the cow is sacred, the wrong way—perhaps not unlike St. Francis's preaching of the Gospel.

FRANCIS COCKTAIL

1 oz. [Beefeater] gin
1 oz. brandy

¼ oz. dry vermouth
¼ oz. Grand Marnier

Stir ingredients in a mixing glass with ice forty times and strain into a cocktail glass.

St. Francis was not as successful in Japan as he was else-where, in part because of the difficulties he had in master-ing the culture and the language. Have a Japanese cocktail to toast St. Francis's valiant efforts. This delicious concoc-tion is a nineteenth-century Western tribute to Japan rather than an authentic Japanese product, much like the Spanish missionary braving the shores of Nippon.

JAPANESE COCKTAIL

2 oz. brandy
1 lime slice or lemon twist
¼ oz. fresh lime juice
  (or 1 dash orange bitters)

1 dash Angostura bitters
¼ oz. orgeat syrup

Pour all ingredients except lime/lemon slice into a shaker filled with ice and shake forty times. Strain into a cocktail glass.

BEER AND BRANDY

St. Francis's base of operations in India was the state of Goa. Goa produces a Kings Black Label premium pilsner, but since it is sold only in that state, turn instead to an Indian beer (p. 66) or to an India Pale Ale, a hoppy and now popular kind of beer (especially among micro and craft brewers) that was originally made in England for export to India.

Lastly, see if you can get your hands on a bottle of feni, a brandy made in Goa from cashew apples.

ST. BARBARA, DECEMBER 4

According to the stories that have come down to us, Barbara (ca. 3rd c.) was a beautiful maiden who was imprisoned by her father in an effort to shield her from the outside world. Barbara nonetheless converted to Christianity while her father was away, and when he returned he handed her over to the authorities, who condemned her to death by beheading. Barbara's wicked father personally carried out the sentence, but on his way home he was struck dead by a bolt of lightning and consumed in flames. One of the Fourteen Holy Helpers, Barbara is invoked against fever and sudden death.

Some sections of central Europe observed a charming custom that gives us an idea for a drink. On St. Barbara's Day, a maiden would break off a branch from a cherry tree and place it in a vase of water. If the branch blossomed on Christmas Eve, she was sure to find a husband within the year. We're not certain how successful this practice is, but it at least affords the opportunity to have a drink with a cherry in it such as an Old Fashioned or a Manhattan (p. 68). And as we said in the introduction, we definitely recommend Luxardo cherries and Toschi amarena black cherries (p. xxiii).

Because of her father's explosive ending, St. Barbara is also the patron saint of armorers, artillerymen, bomb technicians, cannoneers, fireworks manufacturers, gunners, ordnancemen, the U.S. Army Field Artillery, miners, tunnelers, and so forth. For her feast day, then, it's time to bring out the big guns such as a French 75 or an Artillery. Or, you can stick to the basics with a Barbara Cocktail.

ARTILLERY

1½ oz. gin
1 dash Angostura bitters

¾ oz. sweet vermouth
1 lemon twist

Pour all ingredients except lemon twist in a mixing glass with ice and stir until very cold. Strain into a cocktail glass.

FRENCH 75

1½ oz. gin
2 tsp. simple syrup
½ oz. fresh lemon juice

5 oz. brut champagne
lemon twist, cherry, orange
slice (optional garnishes)

Pour gin, lemon juice, and simple syrup into a shaker filled with ice and shake forty times. Strain into a champagne flute or champagne tulip and top with champagne. Garnish with lemon and/or cherry and orange slice.

BARBARA COCKTAIL

1 oz. vodka   ½ oz. cream
½ oz. crème de cacao

Pour all ingredients into a shaker filled with ice and shake
forty times. Strain into a cocktail glass.

BEER AND WINE

If you are hankering for the cherry option, look for any
cherry stout or cherry wheat beer. The Brewhouse Brewery has a Saint Barb's Ale in three strengths (Abbey Ale,
Dubbel, and Tripel), but you'll have to travel to Santa
Barbara, California to taste them.

A more feasible alternative is a wine from California's
Santa Barbara County, so named when the Santa Barbara
Channel was navigated by Spanish explorer Sebastián
Vizcaíno on St. Barbara's feast day in 1602. There are a
number of wineries in the area, including Au Bon Climat,
Laetitia, Meridian, and the Santa Barbara Collection. The
region's peculiar geography and proximity to the Pacific
Ocean give its terroir a lovely distinctiveness.

LAST CALL

Challenge your guests to come up with the worst
possible pun about St. Barbara and her patronage of
things that go boom, and work it into a toast. Praise her for
her caliber, her incendiary personality, her long range, etc.

St. Sabbas, December 5

Also known as Sabbas the Sanctified, St. Sabbas or Sabas (439–532) was born in Cappadocia (present-day Turkey) and entered a monastery at the tender age of eight. The precocious child quickly learned to read and eventually gained a mastery of Sacred Scripture. After twenty-six years of monastic life, Sabbas felt called to live as a hermit in a cave. Five years later, however, his happy solitude was interrupted by disciples who sought him out and asked him to become their abbot. Sabbas obliged and founded the Great Lavra Monastery, now known as Mar Saba, near Jerusalem. All was well until some of the monks began to complain that their abbot was not a priest—as if they didn't know this going in! Sabbas, however, maintained his charity; when the opposition continued even after he was ordained and appointed archimandrite of all the monasteries in Palestine by the Patriarch of Jerusalem, he simply withdrew to another monastery that he had founded earlier.

And as if these disgruntled and ungrateful brethren weren't enough, Sabbas was also vexed by the false brethren known as heretics. A strenuous opponent of the Monophysites and the Origenists, he was not afraid to call on doctrinally-drifting emperors and put them in their place.

In recognition of St. Sabbas's love of the eremitical life (that's the life of a hermit, FYI), enjoy a Solitude Is Bliss cocktail. This tasty winner also makes a great summer drink.

SOLITUDE IS BLISS

By Chris Bostick
1½ oz. Dolin dry vermouth
½ oz. gin
1 oz. ruby red grapefruit
  juice
½ oz. fresh lime juice

¼ oz. chamomile syrup
  (equal parts chamomile
  tea and sugar)
seltzer water
grapefruit wheel or wedge
  lightly dusted with salt

Pour all ingredients except seltzer and grapefruit into a shaker with a small amount of ice and shake forty times. Pour into a highball filled with ice, top with seltzer, and stir. Garnish with grapefruit.

Saint Sabbas was an old monk: not only did he live to the age of ninety-three, but his very name is derived from the Aramaic for "old man." So for something warm on a frosty night, try Old Monk rum, a staple of India since 1954 that is described as having a "thick molasses nose with vanilla notes and a butterscotch bite." Sounds like an angry uncle with a cold, but it goes well in a Rum Toddy, the recipe for which you can steal from tomorrow's Feast of St. Nicholas.

WINE

San Saba, Texas, takes its name from today's saint in a roundabout way: it was named after a mission which was named after Saint Sabbas because Spaniard explorers found the location for the mission on Holy Saturday (Santo Sabado). Whatever the connection, San Saba is now the home of the award-winning Wedding Oak Winery, nestled in the picturesque Hill Country of central Texas. When he was a young man, Sabbas resisted his parents' attempts to marry him off, so be sure to toast the saint with a glass of "Wedding Oak" in a spirit of irony.

LAST CALL

A toast: Through the intercession of the monk and hermit Saint Sabbas, may we live with our family members in peace during this Christmas season—and also get time off from them for good behavior.

ST. NICHOLAS, DECEMBER 6

The titular saint of this book, Nicholas of Myra (270–343) was a bishop in Asia Minor who earned the nickname "The Wonderworker." In A.D. 325 he was one of the orthodox bishops at the Council of Nicaea who defended the divinity of Christ from the Arian heresy. According to one account, Nicholas, unable to bear Arius's blasphemous prattling any longer, walked up to the heresiarch and slapped him. As one clever meme featuring the bishop puts it, "Deck the halls? Try deck the heretic!" A 2004 forensic study of the skull of St. Nicholas (now in Bari, Italy) reveals that the saint's nose was severely broken and reset, so perhaps fisticuffs were not entirely unknown to him after all.

St. Nicholas was as gentle to the poor as he was ferocious to the wolves in sheep's clothing. He saved three sisters from prostitution by throwing bags of money through an open window or down the chimney of their house, enough to give them a dowry for marriage (and to give us the seeds for his gradual transformation into Santa Claus).

On this feast day, try a simple and yummy St. Nicholas' Helper. Or, since St. Nicholas is the patron saint of sailors, have any cocktail made with Grand Marnier ("great mariner") or rum, a seaman's favorite. Depending on the weather tonight, a Rum Toddy might hit the spot. But for the most ancient custom of all, have some *Bischopswijn* or Bishop's Wine, traditionally served in Sinterklaas-loving countries such as Holland on the eve of the feast.

Our friend Peter Kwasniewski has invented two delectable drinks that honor Nicholas at the Council of Nicaea. The color of the Incensed Bishop imitates the deep hue that the saint's otherwise rosy cheeks turned to as he heard Arius dissing the doctrine that the Son of God is consubstantial with the Father. The Anathema Sip, on the other hand, is made with the Greek spirit oúzo to honor the saint's patronage of that country. And with its wordplay on the chilling verdict *anathema sit* ("let him [who disagrees with the Council] be excommunicated"), the drink wins the Best Pun Award in *Drinking with Saint Nick*.

Finally, you can be generous and raise a glass to St. Nicholas's helper—not the drink but the person. In the old country, Krampus is "an ugly, chain-rattling little devil who has to deal with the children who have been naughty" since, as Maria Von Trapp explains in one of her books, "St. Nicholas is much too kind to do the punishing and scolding himself." Likewise, Krampus Herbal Liqueur, which is made by the Chuckanut Bay Distillery in Bellingham, Washington, is a limited release seasonal spirit that works as a devilishly good companion to St. Nick's feast day.

RUM TODDY

1 tsp. sugar   nutmeg
2 oz. rum   hot water
1 lemon slice

Build sugar and rum in an old-fashioned glass or Irish coffee cup. Fill with hot water and garnish with nutmeg and lemon.

ST. NICHOLAS' HELPER

By the "Saints and Spirits" band of brothers at St. John
  Vianney Seminary in Denver, Colorado

1 cup hot chocolate   ½ oz. Rumple Minze
                                     peppermint schnapps

Pour hot chocolate and schnapps into an Irish coffee cup and serve.

BISHOP'S WINE (8-10 SERVINGS)

2 bottles of claret (or a hearty red like Cabernet Sauvignon or Merlot)

2 oranges, quartered and studded with cloves

1 lemon, quartered and studded with cloves

15-20 whole cloves (to be used for studding the oranges and lemon)

2 cinnamon sticks

¼ tsp. allspice (optional)

¼ tsp. mace (optional)

¼ tsp. ginger (optional)

2-4 tbsp. sugar

Pour the wine into a large saucepan. Add the studded fruit and cinnamon sticks and heat slowly for fifteen minutes (do not allow to boil, as this will make the alcohol evaporate). Add the sugar and heat for a minute or two, until dissolved. Strain out the fruit and spices and serve hot.

INCENSED BISHOP

By Peter Kwasniewski

1 oz. gin

1 oz. ruby port

1 oz. sweet vermouth

2 dashes aromatic bitters

2 dashes orange bitters

1 orange twist

Pour all liquid ingredients into a mixing glass and stir forty times. Strain into an old-fashioned glass with ice and garnish with orange.

ANATHEMA SIP

By Peter Kwasniewski

1 oz. gin 1 oz. oúzo (or absinthe)

2 oz. black cherry juice

Pour all ingredients into an old-fashioned glass filled with ice and stir.

BEER AND WINE

The Danish brewery Warwick Bryghus Aps has a Sankt Nikolai Abbey Tripel beer. For wine, Saint-Nicolas-de-Bourgueil is both a village and an appellation in the Loire Valley of France named after an old church dedicated to St. Nicholas. Closer to home, you can try to find St. Nikolaus Bock from Penn Brewing.

LAST CALL

Raise your glass and say, "To the real Santa Claus, scourge of heretics and champion of the poor: may he help us defend the faith and assist the needy."

ST. AMBROSE, DECEMBER 7

We move from one great bishop of the early Church who smacked a heretic to another who smacked down an emperor and an empress. St. Ambrose (340–397) was the Governor of Aemilia-Liguria in northern Italy when he addressed the faithful in Milan as they were electing a new bishop. The crowd suddenly cried out, "Ambrose for bishop!" even though he hadn't even been baptized yet. Ambrose went from being a catechumen to a bishop in a mere nine days. As the chief shepherd of Milan he energetically defended the Church from heresy and imperial encroachment. He browbeat the Emperor Theodosius into doing public penance for a massacre he perpetrated at Thessalonica, and he stared down the Empress Justina by staging a sit-in and refusing to hand over his church to her beloved Arian heretics. Ambrose also found time to receive the great St. Augustine of Hippo into the Church and to compose several magnificent hymns.

Ambrose's symbol in Christian art is a beehive because of the legend that a swarm of bees crawled in and out of his mouth as an infant. Ambrose's nurse was understandably terrified when she saw this, but his father interpreted the event as a sign that Ambrose would one day become a great and eloquent leader.

To honor the honey-tongued Bishop of Milan, have a honeyed spirit. Hidden Marsh Distillery has a Bee Vodka distilled from raw honey. Bärenjäger Honey Liqueur and Bärenjäger Honey & Bourbon hearken to the age of the medieval German *bärenjäger* or bear hunter who used mead-like moonshine to lure their quarry. But the most nominally appropriate choice would be the Polish

Ambrosja or Ambrosia Miodowa Honey Liqueur—if you can find it.

Balcones Distilling Company has a delicious concoction called Rumble, made with local wildflower honey, mission figs, turbinado sugar, and Texas Hill Country spring water. Balcones mixologist Andrew Anderson took a Honeybee cocktail recipe, which is already quite good, and made it even better by adding Rumble. The result: a Rumbling Honeybee. The name also works well for St. Ambrose, who was not afraid to tangle with anyone who opposed the Faith.

Finally, you can honor Ambrose's episcopal see with a Milan cocktail.

HONEYBEE

1½ oz. light rum   ½ oz. honey
¾ oz. fresh lemon juice

Pour ingredients into a shaker filled with ice and shake forty times. Strain into a cocktail glass.

A RUMBLING HONEYBEE

By Andrew Anderson
1½ oz. Balcones Rumble   ¾ oz. honey syrup (2 parts
¾ oz. fresh lemon juice   honey, 1 part water)

Pour ingredients into a shaker filled with ice and shake forty times. Strain into a cocktail glass.

MILAN COCKTAIL

1 oz. bourbon
½ oz. orange juice
1 oz. light rum
1 lemon twist

Pour all ingredients except lemon twist into a shaker filled with ice and shake forty times. Strain into a cocktail glass and garnish with lemon.

BEER AND WINE

McAuslan Brewing in Montreal, Quebec, produces a variety of beers and ales under the label of St-Ambroise. Although they named the label after the street on which they are located, a pious imbiber can direct his thoughts to today's saint (the only problem will be finding a retailer near you who sells them). An alternative is the myriad of honey-flavored beers and ales on the market. We cannot name them all, but we can at least mention some award winners, such as Bogotá Beer Company Cajica Miel, Lovibonds Gold Reserve, Fuller's Organic Honey Dew, and Wychwood BeeWyched.

The wines of Lombardy or Lombardia, the region surrounding Milan, would make a fine contribution to tonight's dinner or festivities. The region is (in)famous for its almost bewildering diversity of grapes and its absence of a dominant signature wine, but don't let that stop you, since diversity does not mean mediocrity. An easy place to start is with the fine sparkling wines produced in the Franciacorta and Oltrepò Pavese areas. Better yet, consult your local vintner.

THE IMMACULATE CONCEPTION OF THE BLESSED VIRGIN MARY, DECEMBER 8

On December 8, 1854, Pope Pius IX solemnly defined what had already been in the Catholic drinking water since time immemorial, namely, that the Blessed Virgin Mary, by a special proactive application of the graces won by her Son's victory on the Cross, was preserved from original sin, thereby making her womb a fitting place for the Son of God and her flesh a fitting source for His. Mary is the only human being besides Adam, Eve, and Jesus Christ to come into this world without original sin, but she is not alone in receiving the graces of the Cross prior to the first Good Friday. *Every* holy person before the Crucifixion, from Abel to John the Baptist, is redeemed by the Blood of the Lamb prior to Its actual shedding by a special preapplication of grace; the only difference with Mary's case is that it was applied to prevent not only actual sin but original.

Given the Blessed Virgin's total purity, who is more worthy of the drink called a White Lady? In *Drinking with the Saints* we offer a simple version of this drink, but under the spiritual direction of our friend Father Robert Johansen we are pleased to present a more sophisticated and delicious variation from the 1960s. Both texture and taste are truly amazing and worth the extra effort.

WHITE LADY

As promoted by its faithful disciple Rev. Robert Johansen

1 egg white	1 oz. Cointreau
1 tbsp. fresh lemon juice	2 tsp. powdered sugar
1 oz. gin	1 dash lemon bitters (optional)
1 oz. vodka	1 lemon twist

Beat the egg white and powdered sugar until firm but not stiff (an electric frother or handheld mixer speeds up the process). Pour the egg mixture and all other liquid ingredients except lemon bitters into a shaker filled with ice and shake forty times. Strain into a cocktail glass and add lemon bitters and lemon twist.

Seven nations are under the patronage of Our Lady of the Immaculate Conception, including the United States. Tonight, pick a classic American cocktail— such as a Martini (p. 42), Manhattan (p. 68), or Old Fashioned (for fancy variations, see pp. 84 and 171)— and dedicate it to Our Lady.

Brazil would also like to help in tonight's celebration, as it too is protected by Our Lady under the title of the Immaculate Conception. And Brazil's greatest achievement in the world of mixology is its national cocktail the Caipirinha (pronounced *kigh-pur-REEN-yah*). This classic is made from a very sweet sugar cane liquor called *cachaça* (pronounced *kah-SHAW-sah*) that is more like an aguardiente than a light rum in its intensity. A higher-end *cachaça* is preferred in making a Caipirinha, since the drink does not disguise the flavor of the main ingredient. If you cannot find *cachaça*, you can do what folks sometimes do in Brazil: substitute it for vodka and have what is called a Caipivodka or Caipirodka.

CAIPIRINHA

| 4-6 lime wedges | 3 oz. cachaça |
| (from ½ lime) | 2 tbsp. sugar |

Muddle the limes and sugar in an old-fashioned glass. Fill with crushed ice, add cachaça, and stir thoroughly.

WINE

Point Concepción Wines in central California is run by the Cargasacchi family, which has been making Italian-style wines in California for five generations. Their winery is named after Point Conception, so called from *La Misión de la Purísima Concepción de la María Santísima*, the Mission of the Immaculate Conception established in nearby Lompoc on December 8, 1787.

LAST CALL

Borrow a page from the Miraculous Medal promulgated by St. Catherine Labouré: "O Mary, conceived without sin, pray for us who have recourse to Thee!"

ST. GORGONIA, DECEMBER 9

Saint Gorgonia (d. 375) came from a remarkably holy family. Both of her parents, Gregory the Elder and Nonna, and two of her brothers, Caesarius and Doctor of the Church Gregory of Nazianzus, were saints. We're dying to know what kind of trouble, if any, three child-saints got into and how two parent-saints responded to it.

Gorgonia has been hailed as "the pattern of a married saint." Her husband was a pagan, but over time she converted him to the Faith. Her children and her

grandchildren grew up to be good Christians, for Gorgonia dedicated not only her soul to God but her whole family and household as well. St. Gregory Nazianzus said of his sister that she combined the best of both the married and celibate states of life, performing her many worldly duties while remaining singularly focused on God, and that so long as she lived she was an example to her family of all that was good. Gorgonia prayed so much that it was as if her knees had taken root in the ground, and she was so "keen of intellect" that both her family and everyone around her treated her counsel and advice as Law. Finally, her brother reports, Gorgonia was so ready for Heaven at the end of her life that she made her last day on Earth "a day of solemn festival with brilliant discourse upon the things above."

Why haven't we heard more about this marvelous saint? They say that St. Jude the Apostle got to be patron saint of the desperate because the similarity of his name to that of Judas the traitor turned everyone off except supplicants who were in the direst of straits. We wonder if a similar plight may have besmirched the legacy of St. Gorgonia, whose name bears an unfortunate resemblance to a snake-haired, stone-making "Gorgon" like Medusa. Even the root of Gorgon/Gorgonia is *gorgos*, the Greek word for "dreadful"—not a good basis, we think, for a girl's name.

So to redeem Gorgonia from undue associations, let's focus on her real beauty, the beauty of her soul. As St. Gregory Nazianzus said in his touching eulogy of her:

> But though she was aware of the many and various external ornaments of women, yet none of them was more precious to her than her own character, and the brilliancy stored up within. One red tint was dear to her, the blush of modesty; one white one, the sign of temperance.

Tonight, to honor the virtuous reddish-white tint of Gorgonia's luminous character, enjoy a Pink Lady.

PINK LADY

1½ oz. gin
½ oz. fresh lemon juice

½ oz. grenadine
1 egg white

Pour all ingredients into a shaker filled with ice and shake forty times. Strain into a cocktail glass.

LAST CALL

If you have some time tonight, read aloud Gregory's eulogy to his sister, which can be found on newadvent.org as "Oration 8" in the writings of Gregory Nazianzus: it's twenty-three paragraphs of sheer eloquence. And be sure to toast to the memory of St. Gorgonia as a model of the married life and holy womanhood. Here is an adaptation of one of St. Gregory's statements about his sister's holiness that can be used as a toast: "To the nature of woman! It can surpass a man's in the common quest for salvation and demonstrate that the distinction between male and female is one of body and not of soul. And may the prayers of the radiant Saint Gorgonia make every one of us, male and female, an example of all that is good."

St. Melchiades,
December 10 (January 10)

St. Melchiades or Miltiades (d. 314) a native of North Africa, was the pope in A.D. 313, the Emperors Constantine and Licinius issued the Edict of Milan that ended the Roman persecution of Christianity.

This calls for a drink! Grappa, the famous Italian pomace brandy made from grapes, is a good choice for a Roman pontiff from North Africa, especially since (according to one legend) it is said to have been invented by a Roman soldier in the Italian town of Bassano del Grappa with distilling equipment that he stole from Egypt. The more accurate account is that grappa is the product of the great Medical School of Salerno in the twelfth century and that the grappa-making process was codified by Jesuits in the seventeenth century—no doubt to fulfill their fourth vow to the pope.

Grappa is now made around the world, although technically the only grappa considered authentic is produced from pomace in Italy or the Italian part of Switzerland or the tiny nation of San Marino. The brandy has several well-known producers including Bepi Tosolini, Berta, Bocchino, Brotto, Distilleria De Negri, Domenis, Jacopo Poli, Nardini, Nonino, Sibona, and Villa de Varda. Usually, unaged grappa is clear while color indicates that it has been aged.

Grappa, which is used in Italy as a *digestivo* to aid in the digestion of heavy meals, can be served neat or in espresso (the latter is called a *caffè corretto* or "corrected coffee"). "Not to take a glass of grappa after an Italian meal," writes Kingsley Amis, "strikes me as the grossest folly."

BLESSED FRANCO GROTTI, DECEMBER 11

If the name Franco Grotti (1211–1291) or its variations such as Francesco Lippi and Frank of Siena conjure up images of a deadly mob boss, you would not be that far from the truth. In the memorable words of one of his biographers, today's saint started out as "a lazy, nasty-tempered teenager who would not obey anyone." A native of the town of Grotti near Siena, Italy, Franco spent most of his time gambling and had to skip town in order to avoid a murder rap. Out of the frying pan and into the fire, Franco then became

a *condottiere*, a leader of a band of mercenaries.

Franco's "lifestyle choices" didn't help his good judgment in other ways, either. At the age of fifty, after losing everything in a game of dice, he is reported to have even gambled his eyes saying, "I will also gamble these to spite Him who made them." God took him up on the bet and immediately struck Franco blind. It was just the prodding that the ruthless criminal needed. Filled with sorrow and regret, Franco vowed to make the famous pilgrimage to Santiago de Compostela in Spain. God rewarded Franco's pledge by giving him back just enough of his eyesight to make the long and arduous journey and, when he arrived at the pilgrimage site, God restored his sight completely.

After several years of living as a hermit, Franco was told during an apparition of the Blessed Virgin Mary to do penance in front of the people of Siena, whom he had scandalized with his great sins. The penitent soldier of fortune obliged by walking through the streets of the city as he whipped himself. At the age of sixty-five, Franco asked to enter the Carmelite order, but the monks told him to try again in five years—they were understandably jittery about his nefarious past. But the monks eventually relented, and Franco spent the last ten years of his life as a Carmelite lay brother, edifying others through his example of penance and humility and even working miracles.

Redemption Rye Whiskey sounds like a good choice for a tough guy who obeyed the call of his Redeemer. Try it in a Blinker cocktail, a vintage Prohibition-era cocktail that is appropriate in a number of ways. The name is a nod to the return of Franco's eyesight, the lemon twist (especially when cut long and narrow) recalls his self-flagellation, and the syrup evokes the raspberry that Franco gave God, so to speak, when gambling his eyes. If you don't like sweet drinks, we suggest reducing the amount of raspberry syrup to ½ ounce.

BLINKER

2 oz. Redemption Rye
¾ oz. grapefruit juice

¾ oz. raspberry syrup
lemon twist

Pour all liquid ingredients into a shaker filled with ice and shake forty times. Double strain into a chilled champagne coupe glass by holding a fine sieve between the shaker and the glass. (Double straining catches any remaining bits of grapefruit pulp.) Garnish with lemon twist.

WINE

Brunello di Montalcino is made in Blessed Franco's neck of the woods, the environs of Siena. The wine is not released until almost five years after harvest, and it often requires at least another five years until its harsh tannins mellow enough for it to be drinkable. How perfect for a man who had to learn patience while he waited to hear back from the Carmelites. And just as Franco became holy during his ten years with the Carmelites, even the most pedestrian Brunellos provide excellent drinking for a decade once they reach maturity.

LAST CALL

A toast: Through the intercession of Blessed Franco Grotti, may we imitate his virtues and avoid his vices.

OUR LADY OF GUADALUPE, DECEMBER 12

We know that you were toasting to the Mother of God a mere five days ago, but so what: Our Lady of Guadalupe deserves her own celebration. The Blessed Virgin appeared attired as an Aztec princess to an Indian convert named Juan Diego on a hill near Mexico City on December 9,

1531. When the bishop asked for proof of the apparition's authenticity, Juan Diego went to the hill and gathered Castilian roses (which are not native to Mexico and were out of season) in his tilma, or cloak. When he unfolded his tilma before the bishop, the flowers fell to the floor, revealing on the tilma a miraculous image of her. Within twenty years, nine million native Americans converted to Catholicism, approximately the same number in Europe that left the Church because of the Protestant Reformation. (Coincidence?) Our Lady of Guadalupe is now revered as the Queen of Mexico and Empress of the Americas, Protectress of Unborn Children, and Heavenly Patroness of the Philippines (possibly because her image was on Spain's first formal expedition to those islands in 1564).

It is time for Mexico to yield up her distilled spirits in honor of her august queen. Rompope is usually enjoyed around this time of year and has the added advantage of having been invented by Mexican nuns, daughters of Mexico who followed Our Lady's example of virginity.

Or, there's tequila and mezcal. The best part about drinking these uniquely Mexican spirits on this feast day is that both are made from the same plant as the fibers of Juan Diego's tilma: the agave. It's like drinking a second-class relic! For tequila, try a Mexico Pacifico, a superior alternative to the margarita; for mezcal, a Mezcalicious on page 55.

Finally, for a domestic tribute—and in honor of the miraculous roses gathered on this day—enjoy a sampling of the venerable Four Roses Bourbon, either neat or in your favorite bourbon cocktail.

MEXICO PACIFICO

1½ oz. tequila   ½ oz. passion fruit syrup
½ oz.fresh lime juice   1 lime wheel for garnish

Pour all ingredients except lime wheel into a shaker filled with ice and shake forty times. Strain into a cocktail glass and garnish with lime wheel.

BEER AND WINE

Enjoy some Mexican beer tonight, served either the way you like it or according to the Mexican custom of a *chelada* (an ice-filled beer glass rimmed with salt and lime on the side) or a *michelada* (the same plus some spicy Bloody Mary or Clamato mix). Corona and Dos Equis are the most common Mexican beers in the U.S., but look for Bohemia and Negra Modelo for an extra treat. Bohemia is made by a brewery named after the Aztec king Montezuma (the Cuauhtémoc-Moctezuma Brewery) and can thus symbolize a gift of the native peoples to Our Lady of Guadalupe.

As for wine, treat yourself to your favorite rosé in honor of the Castilian roses arranged by Our Lady in Diego's tilma. Or, have a bottle from California's Rosemount Estate for the miraculously rose-laden Tepeyac Hill where St. Juan Diego encountered Our Lady and upon which now stands the great basilica housing Juan's iconic tilma. Rosemount's cabernet sauvignon is particularly good, with hints of dark plum and black cherry.

LAST CALL

There is a lingering controversy about the Blessed Mother identifying herself as Our Lady of "Guadalupe." Was she referring to Guadalupe, Spain, which has a miraculous statue of her dating back to Pope Gregory the Great, or is the name a transliteration of the Aztec Nahuatl language for "she who crushes the serpent," a reference to Genesis 3:15 and her victory over the serpent-god adorning the Meso-american temples where human sacrifices commonly took place? Toast to Our Lady, throw back a few, and discuss.

ST. LUCY, DECEMBER 13

Lucy of Syracuse (283–304) was a Christian maiden whose prayers to St. Agatha brought about a miraculous cure to a malady from which her mother was suffering. When the governor of Syracuse found out about her faith, he ordered her to be defiled in a brothel. But the soldiers could not move her an inch, even when they tied her to a team of oxen. They then tried to burn her on the spot, but after getting the wood ready they were unable to light it. Finally, St. Lucy was felled by a sword.

A later tradition also states that Lucy was tortured and that her eyes were gouged out; a different version is that she gouged out her own eyes when a suitor took a lusty interest in them. Either way, Lucy is most famously portrayed in Christian art holding a tray containing her two eyes (actually, we should say two of her eyes, because another pair miraculously grew back). Understandably, she became the patron saint of the eyes and the blind.

Saint Lucia is the name of a distillery in the island country of St. Lucia run by the Renegade Rum Company, which produces limited-edition, artisanal, single-vintage rums. Their 1999 St. Lucia vintage, for instance, consisted of only 1,650 bottles and is supposed to be extraordinary.

An easier option is a *Drinking with the Saints* original—if you can consider a mere rearrangement of ingredients original. The Sancta Lucia Martini is a martini with the olives configured to look like a pair of eyes. We're confident that if Saint Lucy did not have a good sense of humor on Earth, she has one now by virtue of the Beatific Vision and that heavenly mirth which Chesterton says is God's greatest secret.

SANCTA LUCIA MARTINI

2 oz. gin   2 olives
1 dash vermouth

Pour all ingredients except olives into a mixing glass with ice and stir forty times. Strain into a cocktail glass. Transfix the two olives with a cocktail sword so that the pimentos are positioned like eyeballs and place them horizontally on the glass rim.

Another option is a tasty, sweet cocktail called the Lucie.

LUCIE COCKTAIL

¾ oz. fresh lime juice   ¾ oz. light rum
¾ oz. Grand Marnier   ¼ oz. orange curaçao

Pour all ingredients into a shaker filled with ice and shake forty times. Strain into a cocktail glass rimmed with sugar.

WINE

Santa Lucia Highlands is an AVA region that is touted as "California's premier cool-climate winegrowing district." Its fifty wineries and labels include Lucia, Talbot, and J. Lohr.

LAST CALL

Here is an original composition you can sing together—after the throat is duly lubricated, of course. Set to the tune of the catchy "Santa Lucia" (which is about the city of that name in Sicily), it is entitled "Sancta Lucia."

This day we celebrate
A virgin pure and fair,
Lucy of Syracuse,
Filled with a love so rare.

Chorus: Pray for us, blessed saint,
Without God's grace we faint,
Sancta Lucia,
Sancta Lucia.

Beloved by Agatha,
Cure of her mother's pain,
Singing Maranatha,
Christ's bride, cruelly slain. *Chorus*

Now to angelic heights
We praise her name at Mass;
Her soul reflects His light,
Shining like stainèd glass. *Chorus*

Dear patron of our eyes,
Unmoved by soldiers' might,
Graciously hear our cries,
Help us to see aright. *Chorus*

If public singing is not your cup of tea, use the last stanza as a toast.

St. Spiridion, December 14

Spiridion (also spelled Spiridon and Spyridon) lived on the beautiful Mediterranean island of Cyprus from his birth in 270 until his death in 348. A shepherd by trade, he used his humble occupation to remain unseduced by the world's false promises and to grow in holiness. Spiridion was so poor in spirit that he did not even resent people who tried to steal from him. When a gang of thieves came in the dead of night to pilfer some of his sheep, they were seized by an invisible force and kept there until the saint found them in the morning. After praying for their release, Spiridion gave them a ram. Before they left, however, he exhorted them to change their ways and pointed out that they took great risks stealing what he would have gladly given them if they had only asked.

Spiridion was married and had a daughter named Irene, but after the death of his wife he became a monk and the bishop of Trimythous. A persecution broke out, and the Roman authorities gouged out Spiridion's right eye, crippled him, and sentenced him to work in the mines (when you take into consideration St. Lucy's feast on December 13, that's three gouged eyes in two days). Years after the persecution ended, Spiridion attended the Council of Nicaea and was honored as one of the confessors who had suffered for the Faith.

Several miracles are attributed to the saint. A man had asked Spiridion's daughter Irene to store a valuable possession of his, but when Irene died, nobody knew where she had hidden it. Moved with compassion, Spiridion went to his daughter's grave, called her by name, and asked where it was. Irene answered him and disclosed the exact location. If this touching but spooky story does not make you want to have a drink, nothing will.

Spiridion is the patron saint of potters because he once explained how there can be three Persons in One God by holding up a potsherd and noting how it was composed of water, fire, and clay. After giving this explanation, the potsherd suddenly burst into flames, water dripped onto the ground, and dust remained in his hand. This miracle is often seen as a confirmation of Spiridion's wisdom, but we wonder if it wasn't God telling the saint that he could do better when it comes to analogies of the Trinity.

Spiridion is also the patron saint of the Tolstoy family, so your options tonight are to read all of *War and Peace* in a single sitting or to use the book as a doorstop and make yourself a drink.

We can help with the latter. If you are in the mood for a martini, you can modify the Sancta Lucia Martini and use a solitary olive for the saint's remaining peeper (see p. 42). We call it the Single Eye for the Spiridion Guy Martini.

Or if you would rather not transgress the borders of decorum, go with the Cypriot Brandy Sour, the island's unofficial national cocktail. We never made lemon squash before: now, we likey.

CYPRIOT BRANDY SOUR

2 oz. Cypriot brandy (KEO VSOP or Haggipavlu Anglias, or cheat with any grape brandy)
1 oz. lemon squash

2-4 drops of bitters (Angostura or Cypriot Cock Drops brands)
soda water

Build brandy, lemon squash, and bitters in a highball filled with ice. Top with soda water and stir. Lemon squash can be purchased commercially or made with the following recipe:

LEMON SQUASH

4 parts sugar
1½ parts fresh lemon juice

3 parts water

Put sugar and water in a pan and dissolve the sugar by stirring over low heat. When the sugar is dissolved, bring to a boil and cook for about five minutes over high heat or until one-thread consistency is reached (allow the mixture to cool a bit and, taking a dab between your thumb and forefinger, gently pull the dab apart to see if it is like a single thread that does not break). Take mixture off the heat and mix in lemon juice. Store in sterilized airtight bottles.

A cantaritos is a popular cocktail in Mexico named after the signature vessel in which it is served, a small clay pot by the same name (*cantaritos* is a diminutive of *cantaro*, the Spanish word for jug). Spiridion, of course, was not Mexican but the cantaritos jug makes a fitting tribute to his potsherd analogy for the Trinity. You can even smash it afterwards and see if God repeats the same miracle for you.

....

CANTARITOS
....

1½ oz. tequila (reposado recommended)
½ oz. fresh lemon juice
½ oz. orange juice
½ oz. fresh lime juice
salt or worm salt

up to 8 oz. pink grapefruit soda (Q Grapefruit recommended)
1 lime wedge
1 cantaritos de barro clay pot glass

Prepare cantaritos glass by submerging in cold water. Rim the edge with salt—or, for added authenticity, worm salt—by spreading salt onto a small plate and dipping the edge into the salt. Fill the glass with ice and add the tequila and juices. Top off with grapefruit soda and garnish with lime wedge.

Finally, zivania or zivana is not as old as St. Spiridion, but ever since this colorless and grappa-like pomace brandy began to be produced in Cyprus in the fifteenth century, it has been a national favorite. Cypriots especially like sipping zivania on cold nights, but they also use it to treat wounds, colds, and headaches and to massage aching body parts. Sounds like something St, Spiridion could have used after a hard day in the mines.

WINE AND BEER

Commandaria wine may have been named by the Crusaders, but its roots go back to 800 B.C. It also has the distinction of being the world's oldest named wine still in production, so St. Spiridion most likely enjoyed a glass or two now and then in between reforming sheep thieves. Commandaria is an amber-colored sweet dessert wine made on the foothills of the Troödos mountains: available exports include KEO's St. John Commandaria, ETKO's Centurion or St. Nicholas, LOEL's Alasia, and SODAP's St. Barnabas. Commandaria was also popular among the ancient Greeks at religious festivals, so it is high time to baptize it for Christian use (although we suspect that Christian Cypriots have already beaten us to the punch).

As for beer, the Karbach Brewing Company's seasonal ale Yule Shoot Your Eye Out is a clever reference to the classic '80s film *A Christmas Story*, but it can also be repurposed to pay tribute to St. Spiridion's cycloptic sacrifice for the Faith.

LAST CALL

A toast to St. Spiridion: May he help us keep our eye on the prize.

ST. NINO, DECEMBER 15

There are different versions of Saint Nino's name (including Nina, Nune, and Ninny) and different versions of her story. According to a Roman Catholic tradition, Nino was a Christian maiden who was kidnapped and taken as a slave to Georgia—the country, not the U.S. state. But according to most Eastern Orthodox accounts, Nino was part of a prominent Cappadocian family: her father was a general who was related to Saint George and her mother was related to the Patriarch of Jerusalem—moreover, she came to Georgia not unwillingly but out of her own desire to evangelize. Either way Nino, who lived from around A.D. 296 to 340, is now hailed as Equal to the Apostles and the Enlightener of Georgia for her role in converting the Kingdom of Iberia (the ancient name for that region) to Christianity.

Nina's success in Georgia began when she cured a sick infant, a miracle that attracted the attention of Queen Nana, who was also ill. After Nina cured her too, the queen converted. Her husband King Mirian III was a tougher nut to crack, but he too embraced the Faith after he was enveloped in a mysterious darkness (sometimes described as a fog and sometimes as a solar eclipse) during a hunting trip. Praying to "Nino's God," the king vowed to convert if he was rescued, and immediately the darkness was dispelled. Returning home safely, he was soon building a church and asking for clergy from his neighbor the Emperor Constantine. So it was that one woman—and perhaps a poor slave at that—brought a whole country into the light of the Gospels. Talk about rags to riches.

One of Georgia's most popular beverages is *chacha*, a grappa-like pomace brandy that was once mostly homemade but is now available from distillers such as Binekhi—their Chacha Estragon won the silver medal at the 2007 Mundus Vini awards. Georgians also claim that *chacha* is a cure for acne, which would explain St. Nino's clear complexion in all of her icons.

WINE

St. Nino's Cross, a symbol of Georgian Christianity, is also known as a "grapevine cross" because of its sloping arms. Wine, anyone? The oldest evidence of wine-making has been found in Georgia: archeologists recently discovered that wine was being made there in 6,000 B.C. using a method of underground fermentation that is still practiced in that country today. *Food & Wine* suggests a 2016 "Pheasant's Tears Saperavi," which it describes as "earthy and so dark it's almost black"—an appropriate tribute to St. Nino and the "mysterious darkness" that precipitated King Mirian's conversion.

LAST CALL

A toast: May "St. Nino's God" dispel the darkness in our lives.

ST. EUSEBIUS OF VERCELLI, DECEMBER 16 (AUGUST 2)

As if in anticipation of her celebration of the birth of the God-man, the Church celebrates several saints in December who were stalwart foes of Arianism, the heresy that denied that Jesus Christ is true God and true man. One of these early heroes is St. Eusebius (283–371). Born in Sardinia, Eusebius became the Bishop of Vercelli in northern Italy. He suffered greatly for his opposition to the Arian heresy and his defense of St. Athanasius of Alexandria, so much so that the Church traditionally honors Eusebius as a martyr, even though he died an old man in his bed (after years of exile).

WINE

St. Eusebius's home island of Sardinia has more sheep pastures than vineyards, and its wines tend to be "powerfully alcoholic." The Cantina Santa Maria La Palma, however, has made for itself a decent reputation making red, white, and sparkling wines as well as two different kinds of grappa. The saint's adopted home of Vercelli, on the other hand, is located in the outstanding wine region of Piedmont or Piemonte. Vercelli is not a wine-making hub like its sister cities Asti and Alba, so look to the region as a whole in order to quench your thirst. Asti Spumante is a famous Italian sparkling white wine, and the noble red Nebbiolo grape is behind the celebrated DOCGs Barolo and Barbaresco.

LAST CALL

Like the priest does at Mass and like the ancient Romans and Jews used to do, put a drop of water in your glass of wine tonight (or in your whiskey) as a sign of your belief in the hypostatic union of the divine and the human in the person of Jesus Christ. Then, toast to today's saint: "Honor and health to the faithful friends of St. Eusebius, and confusion and defeat to the spawn of Arius!"

ST. LAZARUS OF BETHANY,
DECEMBER 17 (JULY 29)

Not to be confused with Lazarus the beggar, Lazarus of Bethany is the brother of Martha and Mary who was raised from the dead after four days in the tomb. When Jesus learned that His friend had died, He commanded the tomb to be opened. Ever the realist, Martha objected with the reply—in the wonderfully earthy Douay-Rheims translation of the sixteenth century—"Lord, by this time, he stinketh" (Jn. 11:39). Stinketh or no, Jesus prevailed and brought their brother back to life.

An excellent choice for this occasion is a classic cocktail called the Corpse Reviver #2 (there is a #1 as well, but we like this one better). Trust us: it stinketh not. In fact, it was one of our favorite discoveries when we researched *Drinking with the Saints*.

CORPSE REVIVER #2

¾ oz. gin
¾ oz. Cointreau
¾ oz. Lillet Blanc

¾ oz. fresh lemon juice
2 drops (or 1 dash) of pastis
(or absinthe)

Swirl the pastis in a cocktail glass, lining the inside. Pour the other ingredients into a shaker filled with ice and shake forty times. Strain into the cocktail glass.

OUR LADY OF SOLITUDE, DECEMBER 18

As the story goes: "One day during the 17th century, an unattended, heavily-laden pack donkey staggered into Oaxaca and died. No one knew where it had come from, who owned it, or what it carried. When the people examined his pack, they found a beautiful statue of Our Lady of Solitude. She wore a crown of diamonds with a huge drop pearl in the middle, and a black velvet robe with semi-precious stones. The people decided that as the donkey had died at that spot, they would build a church there to house the little statue."

And they did. The Basílica de Nuestra Señora de la Soledad in Oaxaca de Juárez, Oaxaca, Mexico, is a beautiful Baroque church still standing today. Devotion to Our Lady of Solitude had begun earlier in the sixteenth century by Queen Juana after the early death of her husband Philip I and spread throughout the Spanish-speaking world. As you might expect from the donkey story, however, the devotion is particularly strong in Oaxaca, which claims Our Lady of Solitude as its patroness.

What better way, then, to mark this feast day than with mezcal, Oaxaca's most famous libation? Tequila's older and arguably more interesting cousin, mezcal is made from the agave plant, but unlike tequila (which can be mixed with other alcohols) mezcal must be made from 100 percent agave. Mezcal is also generally produced not in large distilleries but in small artisanal batches by roasting the agave in an earth oven, giving it a smokier flavor. The liquor is most famous for having a "worm" in it, but it's actually the larva of a moth that destroys the agave plant, added to enhance the flavor.

Because its smoky qualities render it more of a challenge for use in a cocktail, mezcal is usually drunk neat, sometimes with an orange slice sprinkled with *sal de gusano* or "worm salt"—ground fried larvae, ground chili peppers, and salt. (Remember, Our Lady wants you to be brave.) The worm salt on the orange was a delightful surprise to us, better than the lemon or lime from our college days and more conducive to sipping and enjoying the affordable yet satisfying bottle of Monte Alban mezcal we found.

Mezcal is aged and labeled like tequila, and some of the older mezcals are more like a cognac. And if you insist, you can have mezcal in a cocktail like this one:

MEZCALICIOUS

1 oz. San Cosme Mezcal
  (or any mezcal you can find)
½ oz. Cointreau

1 oz. orange juice
1 tsp. fresh lime juice
worm salt

Rim a cocktail glass with worm salt. Pour remaining ingredients into a shaker filled with ice and shake forty times. Strain into cocktail glass.

BLESSED URBAN V, DECEMBER 19

VRBANVS·V·PAPA·GALLVS

A native of the French region of Languedoc, Urban V (1310–1370) was born Guillaume de Grimoard. William entered the Benedictine Order at the age of seventeen and became a priest, a respected professor of canon law, and a prior. He had a reputation as a reformer with integrity. When several bishops tried to put the financial squeeze on his priory, he defied them; one archbishop even physically assaulted him, but the prior stood his ground. Later the pope had William conduct several important missions in Italy to root out corruption in the Church.

After his election to the papacy, Guillaume (now Urban V) kept up the same good fight. To the disappointment of papal hangers-on, he continued to follow the Benedictine Rule and lived simply and modestly. Urban pressed for reform wherever he could, oversaw the restoration of churches and monasteries, promoted clerical formation and higher ed, and came fairly close to reuniting the Catholic and Orthodox Churches. But Urban was no monkish milquetoast; he excommunicated bad guys and tried (unsuccessfully) to whip up another Crusade against the Turks.

Urban was, however, a bit of a worrywart where public safety was concerned. During one unusually cold winter, he threatened excommunication to anyone who tried walking on the frozen Rhone River, so concerned was he that the ice would break and people would fall in.

Urban's greatest accomplishment would have been moving the papacy back to Rome from Avignon, France, where it had been for several decades. Even though he was a Frenchman, Urban knew that as the Bishop of Rome the pope belonged in the Eternal City and not soaking up the sun in the south of France. With great courage he defied the French crown and moved the papal court back to Rome where he immediately began repairing churches and helping the poor. But troubles persisted, and Urban's health and old age were not helping. Finally, after three years, Urban threw in the towel; under pressure from his French cardinals, he returned to Avignon. The worn out holy pontiff died three months later. It would be another six years before the popes left Avignon for good.

Urban's life is an encouraging reminder that you can louse things up and still be a holy man—a useful lesson to keep in mind should one's holiday plans turn into a version of National Lampoon's Christmas Vacation. Of the six Avignon popes, Urban V is the only one to have made it to the rank of blessed.

We're tempted to make a bad wordplay on the name "Urban the Fifth" and how much whiskey you should drink tonight, but we imagine the austere pontiff would not approve. Instead, let us poke loving fun at his "capricious" decision to move back and forth from Avignon. The Caprice cocktail is a chic concoction that puts an aromatic twist on the classic martini. The Bénédictine honors Urban's religious order, the dry or French vermouth his nationality, and the orange bitters the travails he suffered moving from one Mediterranean location to another (where oranges grow, of course). As for the gin, let's see it as the clear Spirit that moved him to serve the Church.

CAPRICE

1½ oz. gin
½ oz. dry vermouth
½ oz. Bénédictine liqueur

1 dash orange bitters
1 orange twist and 1 cherry
to garnish (optional)

Pour all liquid ingredients into a mixing glass and stir forty times or until very cold. Strain into a cocktail glass and garnish with orange twist and cherry.

WINE

Châteauneuf-du-Pape is your obvious wine choice for tonight. This appellation, which means "the new palace of the pope," is for the wine region where the Avignon papal residence once stood. According to one yarn, when the Italian poet Petrarch asked Blessed Urban V in 1366 why he remained in Avignon, the holy pontiff allegedly replied that the local wines were far superior to anything he could get in Rome. A Châteauneuf-du-Pape Saint Benoît ("Saint Benedict") would offer appropriate homage to Blessed Urban's religious order.

LAST CALL

A toast to Blessed Urban V: because of his successes he deserved a drink; because of his failures he needed one. Either way, may his intercession help us succeed in our efforts at reform both within and without.

ST. DOMINIC OF SILOS, DECEMBER 20

We like how during Advent, as a sort of anticipation of the beautiful Christmas scene at the manger, we meet a couple of shepherd saints along the way. Spiridion, whose feast was on December 14, was a shepherd, and so is today's saint. Dominic (1000–1073) was a Spanish shepherd boy, and in fact the long hours he spent alone minding his sheep in the foothills of the Pyrenees helped him fall in love with prayer and prepare him for life as a Benedictine. Dominic became a good monk and was elected prior of his community. But when the king tried to seize land from his monastery, Dominic resisted him and was subsequently kicked out. A neighboring king let him have a dilapidated monastery called St. Sebastian at Silos and soon Dominic turned the place into a center of learning and liturgy—the Mozarabic liturgy, to be precise, which is a very cool ancient rite with a surreal Arabic kind of chant.

After Dominic's death the monastery was named the Abbey of Santo Domingo de Silos. Almost a century later, Blessed Joan of Aza went to the shrine to pray that God would give her another son. St. Dominic later appeared to her in a dream and told her that she would indeed have a son who would be a shining light to the Church. In gratitude, Joan named the boy Dominic, and it was that boy who grew up to be the great founder of the Dominican Order. As a result of this story, St. Dominic of Silos became a patron saint of pregnancies and pregnant women. From medieval times until 1931, his abbatial crosier was used to bless the queens of Spain and was placed by their beds when they gave birth.

If it's good enough for the Queen of Spain, it's good enough for us. Tonight pay tribute to Dominic's powers of blessing with a Benediction cocktail. The Bénédictine liqueur honors Dominic's religious order, and if you choose Cava sparkling wine instead of champagne, you also honor Dominic's Spanish heritage. But if you don't like your drink too sweet, reduce the Bénédictine to ½ ounce.

THE BENEDICTION

¾ oz. Bénédictine liqueur
dry white sparkling wine
  (champagne or Cava)

1 dash of orange bitters
1 lemon twist

Pour Bénédictine into a champagne flute, add orange bitters, and top with sparkling wine. Garnish with lemon twist.

WINE AND BEER

Saint Dominic came from the region of Rioja, and the wines of Rioja are second only to sherry for being the most internationally recognized of Spanish wines (Rioja wines were also well-appreciated in Saint Dominic's day). Look for them under the appellation Denominación de Origen Calificada, or Rioja DOCa.

As for beer, Schaefer is an American brand that has been around since 1842. The brew was named after the two brothers who founded the company, but its name implicitly honors St. Dominic's first profession: *Schäfer* is German for "shepherd." Or, continue with the blessing theme by tracking down some Benediction beer. A Belgian-inspired abbey double ale from the Russian River

Brewing Company, Benediction has aromatic notes and hints of chocolate, tobacco, and spice with a slightly malty finish.

LAST CALL

A toast: May St. Dominic of Silos shepherd us with his blessings, regardless of whether or not we are expecting.

St. Thomas the Apostle,
December 21 (July 3)

The apostle famous for his doubting is, fittingly, the apostle first to affirm explicitly the divinity of Jesus Christ. After rebounding from his incredulity about the Resurrection, Thomas proclaimed, "My Lord and my God" (Jn. 20:24-29). Along with the December saints who fought the Arian heresy, St. Thomas's belief that Jesus is true God primes the pump nicely for the festival celebrating the birth of the God-man.

St. Thomas is hailed as the Apostle of India because it is believed that he spread the Gospel to that faraway land and created the ancient church called the "St. Thomas Christians." According to one tradition, it was there that Thomas, an experienced carpenter, was commissioned to build a palace for a local king but spent the money instead on the poor so that the monarch would have an eternal abode in Heaven. The king was not pleased with this allegorical application of his expenditures and threw Thomas into jail. St. Thomas escaped and is today the patron saint of architects.

COCKTAILS

You can honor St. Thomas's patronage with a delicious Builder Upper.

BUILDER UPPER

2 oz. fresh lemon juice
1½ oz. cognac
1 oz. Bénédictine

soda water
1 lemon spiral

Build juice, cognac, and Bénédictine in a highball glass filled with ice. Top with soda water and garnish with lemon. Stir before drinking.

To honor Thomas's *name*, look no further than a Tom & Jerry, a classic Christmastide mixed drink that has been around since the 1820s. We figure that if you are only making one or two, you'll want the simplest version possible, but for a larger party it wouldn't take much more effort to have something a little more lavish. We therefore include a recipe for a single or double serving and a recipe for a twelve-drink batter.

General note: The key to a good Tom & Jerry is a stiff batter and a warm mug. You can preheat the mug by pouring hot water in it and then emptying it.

TOM & JERRY

1 egg
1 tsp. powdered sugar
1 oz. light rum

1 oz. brandy
hot water or milk
nutmeg

Separate egg yolk from white. Beat egg white until it forms stiff peaks. Beat egg yolk until it forms soft peaks. Combine both and mix in the sugar. Beat more if necessary.

Pour rum and brandy into a mug or Irish coffee cup and add hot water or milk (about three ounces). Top with batter and sprinkle with nutmeg. Note: you can get away with using this batter on two drinks.

Some places sell a premix batter, but if you'd rather make your own, here is one delightfully decadent recipe.

TOM & JERRY BATTER

12 eggs
½ tsp. salt
6 tbsp. sugar
1 tsp. vanilla

1 tsp. ground nutmeg
1 tsp. ground cloves
1 tsp. ground allspice

Separate the egg yolks from the whites. Beat the yolks until they form soft peaks. Add salt to the whites and beat until they form stiff peaks. Combine the yolks and white with the rest of the ingredients and mix until well blended. The batter makes at least twelve drinks and can be served fresh or refrigerated for several weeks.

To make a Tom & Jerry cocktail from the batter, add 1 oz. of light rum and 1 oz. of brandy to a mug or Irish coffee cup. Add three or more ounces of hot water or hot milk and top with a heaping tablespoon of batter. You can also omit the alcohol and make a tasty Virgin Tom & Jerry.

Another nineteenth-century creation is the Thomas and Jeremiah—a fancier name but a simpler recipe.

THOMAS AND JEREMIAH

1½ oz. light rum
½ tsp. brown sugar

½ oz. fresh lemon or lime juice
hot cider

Build rum, sugar, and juice in a mug or Irish coffee cup and top with hot cider.

BEER AND WINE AND BRANDY

In Norway, when people thought about the Feast of St. Thomas, they thought about beer because December 21 was the last day to brew beer until after Epiphany. As a result, the apostle took on the nickname "St. Thomas the Brewer" as Norwegians visited each other on his feast day to sample each other's Christmas ale.

If you are not a home brewer, look for St. Thomas Black Saison, a solid winter beer made at the Selkirk Abbey Brewing Company in northern Idaho. Or for a taste of the exotic, let St. Thomas's last mission territory provide the beers tonight. India exports several brands to the U.S., including Kingfisher, Taj Mahal, Maharaja, and Flying Horse. Of the four, Flying Horse and Maharaja have the best reputation, although Taj Mahal is not bad with a good curry or tandoori chicken. Kingfisher is produced both in India and in Saratoga Springs, New York: the Indian bottling is considered superior.

As for wine, in order to reach the west coast of India, St. Thomas probably traveled with merchants from Syria who traded in Laodicean wine, considered a delicacy among the kings and upper class of India. "The ancient Indian poets," our friend Dr. Basil Davis informs us, "write about the 'cool and fragrant wine' brought by the Greek-speaking foreigners from across the Arabian sea." Laodicea (in modern-day Turkey) is no longer a going concern, so fill the gap tonight with any Mediterranean wine you can find: Greek, Italian, etc.

For something more indigenous, the region of Kerala in India (where St. Thomas brought the Gospel) has a palm wine called kallu, but it is, alas, next to impossible to find in the States.

LAST CALL

If you are drinking beer, the toast is obvious: "To St. Thomas the Brewer!"

The Gospel mentions the fact that Thomas was also called *Didymus* or "twin" (Jn. 20:24). Some apocryphal works make the bizarre claim that he was the twin brother of Jesus, but we suspect that he is *our* twin, a reflection of our doubts and, hopefully, our turnaround. Tonight, make it a double, accompanied by the following toast: "To our alter ego, St. Thomas the Apostle: may he lead us from our egos to the altar." (The bad word-play goes down better after the second round.)

SAINT FRANCES XAVIER CABRINI,
DECEMBER 22 (IN THE U.S., NOVEMBER 13)

Born Francesca Cabrini, Mother Cabrini (1850–1917) thought that she had a vocation to evangelize China, but when she met with Pope Leo XIII to seek his approval, he advised her to look to the West instead. Italian immigrants were flooding the United States and living in great poverty, spiritual and material. Heeding the pontiff, Mother Cabrini and six other sisters arrived in New York City in 1889, and before long she had established sixty-seven institutions throughout the United States, South America, and Europe.

Although Mother Cabrini's influence was felt throughout the world (even, at last, in China), New York City is particularly in her debt. She founded two hospitals in the metropolis, Cabrini High School in Manhattan, and an orphanage in West Park, New York. For Mother Cabrini, the first citizen of the United States canonized a saint and a great patron of the Big Apple, we recommend an all-American classic: the Manhattan.

MANHATTAN

1½ oz. bourbon   1 cherry for garnish
¾ oz. sweet vermouth

Pour all liquid ingredients into a mixing glass with ice and stir forty times. Strain into a cocktail glass. Garnish with a Luxardo maraschino cherry or Toschi amarena black cherry (to honor Mother Cabrini's birthplace).

Or, to toast Mother Cabrini's heroic virtue, try the slightly drier Perfect Manhattan.

PERFECT MANHATTAN

1½ oz. bourbon   ¼ oz. dry vermouth
¼ oz. sweet vermouth

Pour all ingredients into a shaker filled with ice and stir forty times. Strain into a cocktail glass.

SAINT SERVULUS, DECEMBER 23

Once you hear the story of Saint Servulus of Rome (d. 590), you will be grateful for whatever gifts you receive on Christmas no matter how chintzy or lame. Servulus was afflicted from birth with a palsy that left him completely paralyzed, unable to use his arms or legs or to sit up or turn over on his side without help. Reduced to begging, his mother and brother carried him to the front entrance of St. Clement's Church in Rome, where he lived on the alms of passersby. Servulus was illiterate, but he saved enough money to buy a copy of the Psalms and the Holy Gospels (a small fortune back then); he then had others read passages to him so that he could learn these books by heart and meditate on them constantly. Whatever money he had left over after covering his own basic needs he gave to those poorer than himself. According to Pope St. Gregory the Great, Servulus actually thanked the Lord for his affliction, for it allowed him "to be a victim associated with the pains and sufferings of Jesus Christ," and he was known for singing hymns of praise and thanksgiving. As he lay dying, his friends and family were singing one of these hymns when he suddenly said, "Silence! Don't you hear the great and wonderful music in heaven?" They were his last words. Servulus' remains later emitted a pleasing fragrance known in Catholic theology as the odor of sanctity. He was buried in the very church where he spent his life begging, the great San Clemente.

St. Gregory the Great notes that the behavior of this poor, sick beggar is a rebuke to the healthy and fortunate who do no good and cannot stand the least bit of suffering. But it also reminds us during this busy season of the paramount importance of simply *being* a lover of God, of having a heart untroubled by anxiety, and solicitous only about serving and adoring the Lord.

Like Saint Servulus during his lifetime, we rely tonight on the generosity of Saint Clement; but instead of spare change from the congregants at his church, we turn to drinks from his feast day on November 23. If you're in the mood for a fizzy cocktail, look no further than a St. Clements Gin:

St. Clements Gin

2 oz. gin
¾ oz. orange juice
¾ oz. fresh lemon juice
1 tsp. powdered sugar
 (or try simple syrup)

soda water
1 lemon and/or orange
 wheel

Stir all ingredients except soda water in a mixing glass with ice. Strain into a highball glass filled with crushed ice and top with soda water. Garnish with lemon and orange.

But if the weather outside is frightful, we recommend a *Drinking with Saint Nick* semi-original hot drink. Tasty Other's Amaryllis Aphrodite invented a Super Rich Cointreau Hot Chocolate; we tweaked the amount of dark chocolate, added an even longer name, and threw in some lemon zest, which gives the drink a little more pizzazz and completes the association with Saint Clement (Do you remember "Oranges and lemons / Say the bells of St. Clement's"?) The super-rich qualities of this beverage (apparently dark chocolate qualifies as a guilt-free "super food") call to mind Saint Servulus's abundance of grace. Just remember that when shopping for dark chocolate, look for the right percentage of cocoa (62%-71%) and don't be confused by dark chocolate's other names, such as "plain," "black," "bittersweet," and even "semisweet."

ST. CLEMENT'S SUPER RICH COINTREAU HOT CHOCOLATE HONORING SAINT SERVULUS

¾ cup whole milk
¼ cup heavy cream
2½-3 oz. dark chocolate, roughly chopped (62%-71% cocoa)
¾ oz. Cointreau

1 pinch crushed cloves (or an even smaller pinch of ground cloves)
¼ tsp. lemon zest
whipped cream

Combine the milk and cream over medium heat until it starts to bubble. Remove from heat and add the chocolate, stirring until melted. Stir in the Cointreau, cloves, and lemon zest. Pour into a mug or Irish coffee cup and top with whipped cream.

ADAM AND EVE, DECEMBER 24

 Catholics are sometimes surprised to learn that Adam and Eve, who were not exactly a smashing success in Paradise, went on to live a long life of pious penance and ended their lives as saints. The Byzantine icons of the Anastasis and the Western paintings of the Harrowing of Hell, for example, show Christ descending into Limbo on Good Friday and rescuing all of the just souls destined for Heaven, starting with Adam and Eve—by then an elderly couple. Adam and Eve have never had a feast day in the Western Latin calendars, but in the Byzantine rite of the Christian East their feast falls on December 24, and it is this tradition, believe it or not, that led to the Christmas tree. In the Middle Ages, mystery plays were staged on Christmas Eve day that included a Paradise tree, a tree representing both the Tree of the Knowledge of Good and Evil as well as the Tree of Life from the Garden of Eden (Genesis 2:9). The plays in honor of Adam and Eve were a timely reminder of why God became man in the first place. In the fifteenth century, the Paradise tree was moved from the stage to the homes of the faithful, and thus the Christmas tree was born,

traditionally decorated on Christmas Eve with shiny balls (the fruit from the Tree of Knowledge) and candy canes (the Tree of Life).

An easy way to honor our biblical progenitors is with a drink involving apple: Calvados (see p. 92), apple hard cider, apple brandy, apple wine, apple schnapps, Äpfelwein (German apple cider that is served hot in the winter, cinnamon, cloves, and lemon), and so on. Perhaps the most interesting option is applejack, the first distilled liquor native to North America and a great favorite among the colonists. Usually a blend of apple brandy and neutral spirits that retains the flavor of the apples from which it was made, applejack makes the perfect hot toddy on a cold winter's night.

APPLE TODDY

½ tsp. sugar   hot apple cider
1½ oz. applejack   nutmeg

Put the sugar in a mug or Irish coffee cup. Add hot apple cider, leaving enough room in the glass for the applejack, and stir until sugar is dissolved. Add applejack, stirring again, and sprinkle with nutmeg.

Another option is to enjoy a cocktail named after the First Couple. Here are two examples:

ADAM'S APPLE

1 oz. apple brandy or
   applejack
½ oz. gin

½ oz. dry vermouth
dash of green chartreuse

Put ice in a mixing glass and add ingredients, starting with the chartreuse. Stir well and then strain into a chilled cocktail glass.

ADAM AND EVE COCKTAIL

1 oz. gin
1 oz. cognac

1 dash of fresh lemon juice
fruit garnish

Pour all liquid ingredients into a shaker filled with ice and shake forty times. Strain into a cocktail glass. Garnish with the fruit of one's choice.

BEER AND WINE

The Cathedral Square Brewery in Saint Louis, Missouri, brews a crisp apple ale called Forbidden Fruit.

Finally, since it is Christmas Eve, have what Clarence the angel ordered unsuccessfully at Nick's Bar in the classic movie *It's a Wonderful Life*: "Mulled wine, heavy on the cinnamon and light on the cloves." For options, see Glühwein on page 2 and St. John's Wine on page 115.

Vinsanto each night after Vespers, heightening even more the sense of joy to come. The Church and Refectory combined help us to live the truth of our Faith in body and spirit."

Vin Santo (also called Vinsanto or Vino Santo) is a generic kind of Italian dessert wine linked most closely to the region of Tuscany. Vin Santos are usually white and can range from dry to extremely sweet. Vino Santo, or "Holy Wine," is so called either because it was the wine used for the Mass (sweet white wine being the historic preference) or because fermentation traditionally began around All Saints' Day and bottling during Easter Week. Surely the wine is holy, for a cross is typically found on the casks used for aging.

There are dozens of Italian wineries that make Vin Santo, and some bottlings can run into the hundreds of dollars. Among the most affordable yet delicious options exported to the United States are Villa di Campobello's Il Santo, Villa Puccini's Santo Vino, and Badia a Coltibuono's Vin Santo del Chianti Classico.

THE VESPER

Or second, treat yourself to a week of Vesper martinis. Propagated by Ian Fleming and named after one of his "Bond Girls," it nevertheless hearkens to the Vespers antiphons that are at the heart of the Golden Nights. Plus, it's really, really smooth.

VESPER MARTINI

1½ oz. (3 measures)
   Gordon's gin
½ oz. (1 measure) vodka

¼ oz. (half a measure) Lillet
   Blanc
1 large, thin slice of lemon
   peel

Pour all ingredients except lemon peel into a shaker filled with ice and shake forty times. Strain into a champagne coupe or cocktail glass and garnish with lemon.

Note: Fleming's original recipe calls for shaking, but feel free to stir instead.

O WISDOM, DECEMBER 17

> O Wisdom that came forth from the mouth of the Most High, reaching from one end to the other and ordering all things mightily and sweetly: come to teach us the way of prudence.

The Son of God, who proceeds from the Father, is not just wise; He is Wisdom itself through whom all things were made (see 1 Corinthians 1:24; John 1:3). Wrap your head around that mystery as you sip something in honor of the Word who, before taking flesh, ordered all creation mightily and sweetly. We recommend a Sage Gold Rush Cocktail, which nicely orders its flavors as well as the themes of wisdom (sage to remind us of our sagacious Creator), might (a double shot of bourbon), and sweetness (simple syrup). The gold in the title is also an apt tie-in to the Golden Nights, especially on opening night. Drink too many of these potent potations, however, and you will lose the way of prudence.

Whatever your drink choices during these special weeks, remember: Keep your O, baby.

SAGE GOLD RUSH COCKTAIL

By Brooklyn Supper

2 oz. bourbon

1½ oz. honey sage simple syrup

1½ oz. fresh lemon juice (or 1 lemon)

lemon twist

sprig of sage

Pour all liquid ingredients into a shaker filled with ice and shake forty times. Strain into an old-fashioned glass filled with ice and garnish with lemon twist and sage. And to make the honey sage simple syrup…

HONEY SAGE SYRUP

¼ cup honey

¼ cup water

1 oz. fresh sage leaves, stems removed

Combine honey, water, and sage leaves in a medium saucepan over medium heat. As soon as mixture starts to steam, turn heat off. Steep sage leaves for ten minutes. Strain into a jar or bottle with a lid, pressing leaves firmly to release liquid. Makes about half a cup. Leftover syrup will keep well sealed in the fridge for about one month.

As St. Augustine points out, Christ alone merits the title of Teacher precisely because He is Wisdom itself and the inner Truth we consult anytime we learn. So if whipping up honey sage syrup is too much trouble, try to get on Our Lord's good side with a Teacher's Pet:

TEACHER'S PET

1½ oz. whiskey
½ oz. dry vermouth
1 tsp. sweet vermouth

2 dashes bitters
cherry
orange slice

Build liquid ingredients in an old-fashioned glass filled with ice and stir. Garnish with cherry and orange slice.

WINE AND BEER

Any wine tonight will do, if we can believe the words commonly attributed to Benjamin Franklin, "In wine there is wisdom, in beer there is freedom, in water there is bacteria."

As for freedom, er beer, the Empyrean Brewing Co. in Lincoln, Nebraska has a Winter Wisdom hazelnut brown ale that should do the trick. Or think biblical with Shmaltz's Genesis Dry Hopped Sessional Ale.

O ADONAI, DECEMBER 18

> O Adonai, and Ruler of the house of Israel, who appeared unto Moses in the burning bush and gave him the Law on Sinai: come to redeem us with an outstretched arm.

It is fascinating to consider that not just God but God the Son was present in the burning bush that Moses encountered on Mount Sinai when he was given the Law, even if it was through the mediation of an angel (Acts 7:30). The Bible records that the bush was on fire but not burnt by the flames (Exodus 3:2-4). We can't imitate that miracle, but there are a variety of ways we can put a little fire in our bellies this evening, from slumming it with shots of Fireball Cinnamon Whisky to a satisfying hot toddy variation called a Burning Bush.

But our personal favorite for lighting up this Golden Night is a Smoking Rosemary Old Fashioned, which consists of infusing an old fashioned with the smoke of burning rosemary. Rosemary, that is, "Mary's rose," is linked to the Christmas season by charming folklore (see p. 178). And Spanish peasantry once believed that rosemary "brings happiness on those families who employ it in perfuming the house on Christmas night." A Marian motif is also appropriate for two reasons. First, if God the Son speaks to mankind from the burning bush, then the burning bush is the Blessed Virgin Mary, whose conception and birth of the Messiah were a fiery light that nonetheless did not "consume" her virginity (you can find this interpretation in the traditional liturgy for January 1). Second, December 18 in Spain and elsewhere was traditionally the Feast of the Expectation of the Blessed Virgin Mary; because it falls during the Golden Nights, it sometimes went under the name of "Our Lady of O" or the "Feast of O."

And wait till you see this drink being made! The glowing sprig is like the pillar of fire in which the LORD God dwelled as He led the Israelites to the Promised Land by night, and the smoke from the extinguished sprig is like the cloud in which He likewise dwelled as He led them by day (Exodus 13:24). And when you use Redemption Rye Whiskey in reference to today's antiphon petition to "come and redeem us," you now have a *Drinking with Saint Nick* semi-original concoction: Adonai's Smoking Rosemary Old Fashioned.

BURNING BUSH

1¼ oz. Bushmills Irish
  whiskey
¾ oz. honey

2½ oz. hot water
lemon wedge

Place lemon wedge in Irish coffee cup. Pour whiskey and honey over lemon and top with hot water.

ADONAI'S SMOKING ROSEMARY OLD FASHIONED

2 oz. Redemption rye whiskey
2-3 tsp. simple syrup
2 dashes Angostura bitters
1 sprig of dried rosemary
  (if you only have fresh
  rosemary, throw it in the
  oven or toaster oven for
  4-5 minutes at 350°)

Luxardo maraschino or Toschi amarena black cherry
  (nothing but the best for
  Yahweh!)
fresh rosemary for garnish
  (optional)

Build whiskey, simple syrup, bitters, and cherry in an old-fashioned glass filled with ice and stir. Take the rosemary and light it on fire. Hold it directly over the glass without putting it in, and cover it with a metal shaker, sealing the glass with the shaker. Count to ten: the flame will go out and the drink will be infused with a strong smoky flavor. Remove the shaker and burnt rosemary and, if you wish, garnish with fresh rosemary.

Note: Some folks prefer this drink with a cocktail straw, as there may be burnt rosemary leaves floating on the surface. Your call.

WINE AND BEER

Burning Tree Cellars (close enough) produces small batches of fine wine out of Cottonwood, Arizona. As for beer, the Lost Abbey has a Ten Commandments beer for the Law given on Mount Sinai, but it is a midsummer ale. You may also have trouble finding a brew from Redemption Craft Brewery in London, but it would be fun to try one of their Trinity Light Ales. It will be easier to find Shmaltz's Hop Manna IPA, Golden Road Brewing's Burning Bush Smoked IPA, or Russian River Brewing Company's Redemption Blond Ale.

O ROOT OF JESSE, DECEMBER 19

> O Root of Jesse, who standest for an ensign
> of peoples, before whom kings shall shut their
> mouths and the nations shall pray: come to
> deliver us, and tarry not already!

Jesse was the father of King David, from whose house the Messiah was promised to come.

In Isaiah 11:1 it is predicted that "there shall come forth a rod out of the root of Jesse, and a flower shall rise up out of his root." The traditional interpretation of this verse is that the rod is the Blessed Virgin Mary and the flower is Jesus. (And incidentally, this biblical verse is also the inspiration for mapping out our genealogy as a "family tree.")

But in Isaiah 11:10, Jesus is also addressed as the *root* of Jesse, "who standeth for an ensign of peoples" and whom "the nations shall beseech." Alpha and Omega, we guess. So tonight, to honor Christ as the Root of Jesse, think roots and tubers. Corbin Cash Barrel Reserve Sweet Potato Liqueur is made from 100 percent California sweet potatoes and aged in American white oak. The liqueur works nicely as the alcoholic ingredient in an Irish Coffee.

Vodka, on the other hand, can be made from just about anything, but one of the more traditional options is the potato. Potato vodkas include Karlsson's Gold Vodka, Woody Creek Colorado Vodka (made from Colorado potatoes), Grand Teton Potato Vodka (made from Idaho potatoes), Boyd & Blair (made from Pennsylvania potatoes), Chopin Potato Vodka, Blue Ice, Cirrus, and Vikingfjord.

Isaiah also describes the Messiah as an "Ensign" for the different peoples or nations of the world—not that Christ is a lesser naval officer holding an ensign, but that He is the Ensign itself: while Christians are called to be standard-bearers, Christ *is* the Standard who, when lifted up high on the Cross, shall draw all men to Himself (see John 12:32). To celebrate this awesome mystery, grab an affordable bottle of Ensign Red, a Canadian blended whisky. Ensign Red was named after Canada's old flag before the Maple Leaf took over, but let us baptize this booze and think instead of Our Lord's Sacred Heart as an Ensign for the nations. You can combine Ensign Red with another drinkable root—ginger—in a *Drinking with Saint Nick* original cocktail called The Peoples' Ensign that is inspired by the Moscow Mule and the Irish Ale Cocktail.

Continuing with our radical motif, carrots and beets (both of which are considered roots) go well together in a Taproot cocktail, a drink so nutritious that you might want a second round just for your health. You can also substitute the Bulleit Bourbon with Ensign Red whisky for added piety.

THE PEOPLES' ENSIGN

2 oz. Ensign Red whisky   3 lime wedges
3 oz. ginger beer   1 carrot slice for garnish

Fill a highball glass with ice. Squeeze in the lime and then pour in the whisky. Top with the ginger beer and stir gently. Garnish with carrot to symbolize the root of Jesse.

TAPROOT

By Serious Eats

1½ oz. Bulleit bourbon

1 oz. Carpano Antica sweet
    vermouth

½ oz. beet juice

½ oz. carrot juice

¼ tsp. balsamic vinegar

1 carrot slice for garnish

Pour ingredients into a shaker filled with ice and shake forty times. Strain into an old-fashioned glass filled with ice. Garnish with carrot to symbolize the root of Jesse.

WINE AND BEER

Root: 1 Wines from Chile are "crafted exclusively from grapes grown on original, ungrafted root systems. This purity from root to wine results in pure fruit aromas and a rich finish in every glass of Root: 1." You can challenge this statement from the winery, if you wish, by sampling one of their bottles as you toast to the Root of Jesse. Root: 1's Heritage Red bottling would be a particularly appropriate way to commemorate Jesus' family tree.

As for beer, Hurry Hard Amber Lager out of Ontario, Canada may be the only brew in the world exclusively dedicated to the game of curling, but it can be coopted tonight for our plea that the Messiah hurry up and come. Better yet, Farmington Brewing Company in Michigan makes an India Pale Lager called Hopperation: Hurry Up And Wait—an apt description of the Christian expectation for the Lord's coming.

Root beer is a good option for the little ones and for those abstaining from the strong stuff. But for the adamantly alcoholic, there is fermented or hard root beer such as Not Your Father's Root Beer or Coney Island Hard Root Beer.

O KEY OF DAVID, DECEMBER 20

> O Key of David, and Scepter of the house of Israel, Thou that openest and no man shutteth, Thou that shuttest and no man openeth: Come and liberate the prisoner from prison, sitting in darkness and in the shadow of death.

Drawing from Isaiah 22:22 and 42:7, we reflect tonight on Christ as the Key from the house of David that perfectly fits the locks of our fallen human condition. He opens the door that no man can shut and shuts the door that no man can open and is therefore the only One who can free us from our dark prison. But how? Isaiah again provides the answer:

And I will lay the key of the house of David upon his shoulder: and he shall open, and none shall shut: and he shall shut and none shall open. And I will fasten him as a peg in a sure place, and he shall be for a throne of glory to the house of his father (Is. 22:20-23).

In other words, the key is the Cross, placed first on the Messiah's shoulders and then used to "peg Him in a sure place" so that He can open and shut what no mortal can— Heaven and Hell. Chilling but beautiful.

Key lime, so named from its association with the Florida Keys, is one of the few foods with the word "key" in it. We're taking one of our favorite lime cocktails, the Mexico Pacifico, and rekeying it with key lime juice to produce (drumroll please) a Key of David. The passionfruit syrup is also a good reminder of the Cross, for the passionflower (*passiflora*) was given its name by sixteenth-century Jesuit missionaries to Mexico in honor of Our Lord's Passion.

KEY OF DAVID

1½ oz. tequila   ½ oz. key lime juice
½ oz. passion fruit syrup

Pour all ingredients into a shaker filled with ice and shake forty times. Strain into a cocktail glass.

Note: Key lime can be sweeter than regular (Persian) lime, so you may want to lessen the sweetness by using ¼ oz. key lime juice and ¼ oz. regular lime juice instead.

WINE AND BEER

As we mentioned in the introduction to this chapter, tonight is the night in the monasteries that Brother Cellarer used his key to bring out the best wine. Go and do likewise with your cellar or wine rack.

For something more specific, a bottle of wine that relates to keys would work, like the Sangiovese-based wine called "La Chiave" (the key) that is produced by the Castagna Winery in Australia.

As for beer, anything from Key Brewing in Dundalk, Maryland would be fitting; their Helles Lager comes particularly recommended, so perhaps we could play on the word "Helles" and think of the Key who liberates us from the hell of prison. Other options include a Scepter IPA from Draught Works in Montana and a Shadow of Death Imperial Stout from South Carolina's Snafu Brewing. A few of these and you'll fear no evil.

O DAYSPRING, DECEMBER 21

> O Dayspring, Splendor of everlasting light and Sun of justice: come and shine on them that sit in darkness and in the shadow of death.

Christ is called the *Oriens* or Orient (translated here as Dayspring) in reference to Zechariah 3:8, for He is the Sunrise whose coming dispels our "darkness and the shadow of death," a phrase found several times in the Bible (see Isaiah 9:2; Psalm 106:10,14; Luke 1:79). And Christ, as we learn from Hebrews 1:3 and Malachi 4:2 respectively, is the Splendor of the Father and the Sun of Justice. December 21 is also the winter solstice, when the daylight begins its slow re-conquest of the long nights. Coincidence?

A Tequila Sunrise is the most popular drink named after the dawn, but there are others as well. The Golden Hour, invented by bartender Tanner Dimmick in Lafayette, Louisiana, is made not with tequila but mezcal, and it also contains the magnificent Catholic liqueur chartreuse. And the Golden Dawn, which was judged "The World's Finest Cocktail" in 1930 by the United Kingdom Bartenders' Guild, includes Calvados, an apple brandy from Normandy, France with a circuitous Catholic pedigree—it is named after one of the unfortunate ships from the Spanish Armada that washed ashore after the big storm. Plus, the "golden" in the cocktail's name pays homage to this fifth Golden Night we are celebrating.

Or, honor the Messiah our *Oriens* with a classic Oriental cocktail. Hailed as a "surprisingly sophistical tipple," the drink was allegedly made in 1924 by an American in the Philippines who gave this recipe as a token of gratitude to the doctor who saved his life. We can give ourselves an Oriental tonight with the same spirit of gratitude towards our Divine Physician who drives away our unhealthy shadows.

And since December 21 in the traditional calendar is also the feast of St. Thomas the Apostle, and since St. Thomas is the Apostle of India, *and* since India is east of us, you can turn to the doubting disciple for additional drink ideas (see p. 63).

Tequila Sunrise

4 oz. orange juice
2 oz. tequila

2 oz. grenadine

Stir the orange juice and tequila in a mixing glass with ice and strain into a highball glass. Add ice. Pour in grenadine slowly around the inner perimeter of the glass. The grenadine will settle to the bottom and create a sunrise effect. (But don't forget to stir before drinking.)

Golden Hour

By Tanner Dimmick
1 oz. mezcal (Rey Campero recommended)
1 oz. St. Germaine

1 oz. yellow chartreuse
1 oz. fresh lemon juice
mint for garnish

Pour all liquid ingredients into a shaker filled with ice and shake forty times. Strain into an old-fashioned glass with ice and garnish with mint.

Golden Dawn

By T. Buttery
¾ oz. gin
¾ oz. Calvados brandy
¾ oz. apricot brandy
  (preferably Marie Brizard)

¾ oz. orange juice
¼-½ oz. grenadine
1 cherry for garnish

Pour all ingredients except grenadine and cherry into a shaker filled with ice and shake forty times. Strain into a cocktail glass and drop a stemless cherry with no pick into the drink. Dribble a little grenadine into the drink around the inner perimeter of the glass and allow it to settle to the bottom to create a sunrise effect. After admiring the sunrise, stir gently before drinking—unless you don't mind a dry beginning and a very sweet finish.

ORIENTAL

1 oz. rye
½ oz. sweet vermouth

½ oz. orange curaçao
½ oz. fresh lime juice (or less)

Pour all ingredients except into a shaker filled with ice and shake forty times. Strain into a cocktail glass.

WINE AND BEER

The Tomoka Brewing Co. in Port Orange, Florida, makes a Hefeweizen called Hazy Sunrise Wheat Ale, but it may be difficult to find in the winter.

Finally, since the antiphon repeats the phrase "shadow of death" from the night before, you have our permission to return to Snafu Brewing's Shadow of Death Imperial Stout. Or broaden your imagination and have schwarz-bier, which is German for "black beer." Out of these ominous liquid shadows comes a surprisingly light flavor and body with less than 5 percent ABV. Köstritzer is a common brand and is quite delicious.

O KING OF THE NATIONS, DECEMBER 22

> O King of the nations, and the Desire thereof!
> O Cornerstone that makest both one: come
> and save mankind, whom Thou hast fash-
> ioned from the slime of the earth.

This antiphon reminds us of the English title for the last movement of Bach's beautiful cantata BWV 147: "Jesu, Joy of Man's Desiring." Jesus is indeed the delightful consummation of our deepest longings, or as tonight's antiphon puts it, the Cornerstone who unites Himself to our desire for Him (Isaiah 28:16). And, of course, Christ is the Cornerstone who unites humanity and divinity in His one Person as well as being the Cornerstone of the Church (Eph. 2:20).

Calling Christ the Desired One of the nations, which is taken from Haggai 2:7, eloquently recognizes that all nations and cultures are groaning in some way for the truth, goodness, and beauty that is Christ. But this groaning is not enough; mankind needs a Savior, and so we turn to the One who "fashions man from the slime of the earth." This phrase is an echo of Isaiah 64:8, which compares God's creation of humanity to a potter working with clay. Our antiphon tonight, however, amps things up a bit by speaking of slime or mud rather than clay and thus brings us to the creation of man in the Book of Genesis. Come and save us, we say somewhat boldly to Jesus Christ tonight, because after all, You created us in the first place!

Rather than drinking something made from slime or mud, turn to the Cantaritos: we mentioned it for the feast of St. Spiridion, but it can do double duty in honor of tonight's pottery metaphor (see p. 47). Or make yourself and your friends a Rex Regum (King of Kings), which in *Drinking with the Saints* we offer for the Feast of Christ the King and which we replicate here. The Crown Royal recalls Our Lord's kingship, and the Drambuie is steeped in Catholic history (the recipe to Drambuie was supposedly given to its current producers in 1746 by "Bonnie Prince" Charles Stuart, Catholic claimant to the English throne and grandson of the last Catholic king of Great Britain, James II). Lastly, pomegranate, from which the best grenadine is made, is a symbol of self-giving—perfect for our sacrificial King.

You can also take up the pottery motif by quaffing a liquor associated with clay, such as mezcal and tequila, which are traditionally distilled in clay pots. Tequila and mezcal cocktail options include the Mexico Pacifico (p. 39), Key of David (p. 90), Tequila Sunrise (p. 93), Mezcalicious (p. 55), Golden Hour (p. 93), and Gifts of the Magi (p. 176).

And since tonight alludes to the creation of Adam and Eve, you can also turn to the cocktail suggestions for December 24, the unofficial feast of our first parents (see p. 73).

Other parts of tonight's antiphon can be equally inspiring. Ripe for repurposing, the Cornerstone cocktail was so named because its ingredients unite the drinking cultures of Brazil and Argentina: Brazil is represented by the sugar-cane liquor called cachaça and Argentina by the bitter Italian herb Fernet-Branca, a favorite in that land. Novo Fogo recommends its own Barrel-Aged Cachaça, which has hints of banana bread, chocolate, and coffee (yum!). Hibiscus grenadine may be difficult to track down, but BG Reynolds has a "Lush Grenadine Syrup" made with trace amounts of dried hibiscus, and the Internet has recipes for making your own. We cheated and used regular grenadine, which worked just fine: just make sure to use a grenadine made out of real pomegranate (double-check the ingredients on the label). And if you can't find a proper Brazilian cachaça, look for any aguardiente from south of the border. Finally, whatever you do, don't overdo it on the Fernet-Branca, which leaves a distinctive bitter aftertaste that some like and others abhor.

REX REGUM

1¾ oz. Crown Royal
  Canadian whisky
½ oz. Drambuie

¼ oz. grenadine
¼ oz. fresh lemon juice

Pour all ingredients into a shaker filled with ice and shake forty times. Strain into a cocktail glass.

THE CORNERSTONE

By Novo Fogo

**2 oz. Novo Fogo Barrel-Aged
  Cachaça**
½ oz. hibiscus grenadine

¼ oz. Fernet-Branca
2 dashes orange bitters
orange twist

Pour all liquid ingredients into a mixing glass with ice and stir forty times. Strain into a chilled cocktail glass and garnish with orange twist.

WINE AND BEER

Cornerstone Cellars Winery in Napa Valley may also be able to make you one with what you desire with its impressive array of red, white, and rosé wines.

King Estates Winery in Oregon, on the other hand, is a good choice for honoring Our Lord's reign. Or be less literal and consider a Barolo wine, which the Italians call "the king of wines and the wine of kings." Produced in a region of Piedmont, Italy from native Nebbiolo grapes and traditionally aged in Slovenian casks called *botti* for a minimum of three years and sometimes for over a decade, Barolo wines are the product of patience, the kind of patience folks in Old Testament times needed for Christ's First Coming and the kind of patience we need today for His Second. But as with a Barolo wine (which can also be stored in your cellar for a decade or more), the wait is worth it.

As for beer and Christ's royal title, if you are insufficiently moved by Budweiser's claim to be the "King of Beers" and unable to find King's Beer from India or King Beer from Cameroon, see what your domestic micro or craft brewers can do for you tonight. Candidates include Jester King Brewery's Noble King Hoppy Farmhouse Ale, 3 Floyds Brewing Company's Alpha King American Pale Ale, and Real Ale Brewing Company's Red King Imperial Red Ale.

You can also play in the mud like the LORD God on the sixth day of Creation with a bottle of Mississippi Mud Black & Tan Beer from Mississippi Brewing.

Finally, Emmanuales, now part of the Sheffield Brewing Company in England, has "been brewing beers of biblical proportions since 2014 A.D." They have a line of cleverly named offerings including a dark brown porter called "As the Deer Pants for the Porter" that, playing on Psalm 42:1, nicely evokes tonight's theme of diving longing.

O EMMANUEL, DECEMBER 23

> O Emmanuel, our King and our Law-Giver,
> Expectation of the nations, and their Savior:
> come to save us, O Lord our God.

King, Law-Giver, Expectation/Desire of the nations, Savior: one way or another, all of these titles have already been given to Our Lord during the Golden

Nights. What is new is the latest clue about the Messiah: He will be "Emmanuel," which means "God is with us." The word comes from Isaiah 7:14: "Therefore the Lord himself shall give you a sign. Behold a virgin shall conceive and bear a son, and his name shall be called Emmanuel." God is indeed with us when He comes to us in the flesh, and so it is appropriate on this last Golden Night to recall the prophet's anticipation of the Incarnation soon before we commemorate His birth at midnight on Christmas.

The sibling team of Kate and Drew Trgovac on their website A Bitter Spirit have made a nice contribution to tonight's merriment with their original cocktail O Come O Come Emmanuel. Kate and Drew wanted to honor the O Antiphons' monastic heritage with the Carthusians' unbeatable liqueur chartreuse. They also chose genever gin (pronounced *yuh-NAY-ver*), aka jenever, Hollands gin, Geneva gin, and Schiedam schnapps. Genever is the Dutch precursor to the more common London dry gin (what most Americans think of when they think of gin), but because of its almost whisky-like characteristics, some people put it in a separate category of spirit. Since we couldn't track down a bottle of genever, we used regular (London dry) gin for the Trgovacs' cocktail and were still pleased with the result. And since we're playing fast and loose with other people's recipes, why not try the O Come O Come Emmanuel Cocktail with Ransom Spirits' award-winning Old Tom Gin? Not only is it a great gin in its own right (and technically different from both London dry gin and genever), but the Ransom label ties in nicely with the verses: "O Come, O Come Emmanuel/ And ransom captive Israel."

O COME, O COME, EMMANUEL COCKTAIL

By Kate and Drew Trgovac

2 oz. vodka (preferably Grey Goose)	1 tsp. light crème de cacao
1 oz. genever gin	1 splash of green chartreuse
	2 cocoa nibs

Pour chartreuse into a cocktail glass and coat sides of glass. Pour out (or drink!) excess. Combine vodka, genever and crème de cacao into a shaker filled with ice and shake forty times. Strain into cocktail glass and garnish with cocoa nibs.

Note: You may want to stir this drink instead to avoid bruising the gin.

BEER AND WINE

Salvator Beer was designed for Lent, but with a name like *Salvator* (Latin for "Savior"), it is difficult not to reach for one tonight. The same goes for the Russian River Brewing Company's Salvation Strong Dark Ale and Avery Brewing's outstanding Salvation, billed as the "Holy Trinity of Ales." Or look for the Shmaltz Brewing Company's Messiah Nut Brown Ale, which is produced under the clever brand label He'Brew. But the most nominally appropriate beer goes to Emmanuales (see p. XX) and their pale ale made from malt rye called Ryejoice.

As for wine, your best bet is to return to the "Ransom captive Israel" motif. The aforementioned Ransom Spirits produces a number of organic wines from Oregon grapes, and there are a number of wines from Spanish-speaking countries with "Mercedes" in the title. "Mercedes" is from a Spanish title for the Blessed Virgin Mary (María de las Mercedes) that means "Mary of Mercies," but the word here for mercy is derived from *merces*, the Latin word for a ransom. J. Bouchon has a line of Chilean red wines called Las Mercedes, and the Spanish winery Mercedes Eguren produces several well-regarded wines including a 100 percent cabernet sauvignon bottling that is unusual for Spain but very nice nonetheless.

LAST CALL

Whether you are drinking Vin Santo, a Vesper Martini, or a specialized beverage, be sure to use the Antiphon of the day as your toast and to belt out the corresponding verse from the hymn "O Come, O Come Emmanuel," which we have reorganized here in the order of the O Antiphons

DECEMBER 17

Veni, O Sapientia,	O come, O Wisdom from on high,
Quæ hic disponis omnia,	Who orders all things mightily,
Veni, viam prudentiæ	To us the path of knowledge show,
Ut doceas et gloriæ.	And teach us in her ways to go.
Gaude, gaude Emmanuel	Rejoice! Rejoice! Emmanuel
Nascetur pro te, Israel.	Shall come to thee O Israel.

DECEMBER 18

Veni, veni Adonai,	O come, O come, Thou Lord of might
Qui populo in Sinai	Who to Thy tribes, on Sinai's height
Legem dedisti vertice,	In ancient times did'st give the Law
In majestate gloriæ.	In cloud and majesty and awe.
Gaude, gaude Emmanuel	Rejoice! Rejoice! Emmanuel
Nascetur pro te, Israel.	Shall come to thee, O Israel.

DECEMBER 19

Veni, O Jesse virgula,	O come, Thou rod of Jesse, free
Ex hostis tuos ungula,	Thine own from Satan's tyranny;
De specu tuos Tartari	From depths of hell Thy people save,
Educ, et antro barathri.	And give them vict'ry o'er the grave.
Gaude, gaude Emmanuel	Rejoice! Rejoice! Emmanuel
Nascetur pro te, Israel.	Shall come to thee, O Israel.

DECEMBER 20

Veni, clavis Davidica,	O come, Thou Key of David, come,
Regna reclude cælica,	And open wide our heavenly home;
Fac iter tutum superum,	Make safe the way that leads on high,
Et claude vias inferum.	And close the path to misery.
Gaude, gaude Emmanuel	Rejoice! Rejoice! Emmanuel
Nascetur pro te, Israel.	Shall come to thee, O Israel.

DECEMBER 21

Veni, veni, O Oriens,	O come, O Dayspring, come and cheer
Solare nos adveniens:	Our spirits by Thine advent here,
Noctis depelle nebulas,	And drive away the shades of night,
Dirasque noctis tenebras.	And pierce the clouds and bring us light.
Gaude, gaude Emmanuel	Rejoice! Rejoice! Emmanuel
Nascetur pro te, Israel.	Shall come to thee, O Israel.

DECEMBER 22

Veni, veni, Rex Gentium,	O come, Desire of nations, bind,
Veni, Redemptor omnium,	In one the hearts of all mankind;
Ut salvas tuos famulos	Bid Thou our sad divisions cease,
Peccati sibi conscios.	And be Thyself our King of peace.
Gaude, gaude Emmanuel	Rejoice! Rejoice! Emmanuel
Nascetur pro te, Israel.	Shall come to thee, O Israel.

DECEMBER 23

Veni, veni, Emmanuel,	O Come, O Come, Emmanuel
Captivum solve Israel,	And ransom captive Israel
Qui gemit in exilio,	That mourns in lonely exile here
Privatus Dei Filio.	Until the Son of God appear.
Gaude, gaude Emmanuel	Rejoice! Rejoice! Emmanuel
Nascetur pro te, Israel.	Shall come to thee, O Israel.*

* Translation from *Hymns Ancient and Modern* (1861).

The Twelve Days of Christmas
The Calendar

FROM DECEMBER 25 TO JANUARY 5

I n the modern era, Christmas revelries begin almost immediately after Thanksgiving, continue through December, and crescendo on Christmas Eve and Christmas Day. Partyers then take a break from raising Cain and return to work for a week before donning little pointy hats and popping champagne on New Year's Eve. The day after, America greets the new year with a hangover and waits until Mardi Gras or St. Patrick's Day before living it up again.

But it was not always so. At the height of Christendom Christians preferred restraining themselves during Advent and then making merry during the entire "Twelve Days of Christmas." This duodenary unit of time, which goes back to at least the fifth century A.D., is framed by two outrageous events: the birth of the God-man on Christmas and His manifestation to the Gentiles on the Feast of the Epiphany. It's not every day that the Creator decides to become a creature to save mankind from itself, and so in giddy imitation of this extraordinary inversion, medieval Christians refrained from work during the Twelve Days and observed a number of "topsy-turvy" customs that upended the usual hierarchy of master and servant, parents and children, clergy and laity, men and women, and human and animal. Socially upheaving practices included those of the Boy Bishop, the Lord of Misrule and the Abbot of Unreason, the Feast of the Ass, and the cross-dressing Twelfth Night.

It would be ideal if we could all take off from work from December 25 to January 6 (Epiphany included) to revive this communal celebration, but even if you don't have the luxury of an extended personal leave in order to obey a Lord of Misrule or celebrate all the donkeys mentioned in the Bible (the Feast of the Ass), you can still capture some of the original Christmas spirit during this time by a series of warm-hearted and perhaps even zany evening get-togethers.

And, of course, we're here to help. In this chapter, we offer topical drink ideas for each of the Twelve Days of Christmas based on the feast days that fall therein.

CHRISTMAS DAY, DECEMBER 25

> And Mary brought forth her firstborn son, and wrapped him up in swaddling clothes, and laid him in a manger; because there was no room for them in the inn (Lk. 2:7).

The great Feast of the Nativity of Our Lord Jesus Christ has long served as an occasion for special drinks.

In the Latin countries of Europe, wine is customarily enjoyed on this day, and in the northern countries beer or ale; indeed, a multitude of the latter are now named after Christmas (see below). Traditional drinks with more of a kick include Mexican rompope (p. 38) and a Tom & Jerry (p. 64).

But special mention must be made of eggnog and Christmas punch. Eggnog has been a popular Christmas drink in the English-speaking world for at least two hundred years. Eggnog mix is widely available at Christmastime in grocery stores and supermarkets. It is either served without alcohol or with a shot of brandy (1½ oz.), and always with a sprinkle of nutmeg. Some folks use a combination of brandy and light rum, and some make their own eggnog from scratch according to different recipes with various degrees of complexity. Here is a simple recipe for a single serving, together with the brandy/rum variation.

EGGNOG

1 egg	1 oz. brandy
1 tsp. sugar	½ oz. light rum
1½ oz. milk or cream	nutmeg

Beat egg, sugar, and milk or cream until smooth and frothy. Pour into an old-fashioned glass and add brandy and rum. Stir and top with sprinkled nutmeg.

Christmas punch is the successor of "Wassail," which is a medieval combination of hot ale or mead, roasted apples, eggs, nutmeg, and floating pieces of toast. Today's Christmas punch, by contrast, typically uses wine as the base ingredient. Lamb's Wool, which we recommend for Epiphany, is a variation of the classic wassail but with wine (p. 175).

Below are two Christmas punch recipes from Maria Von Trapp, whom we consult frequently during these twelve days of Christmas. Immortalized by Julie Andrews in the *Sound of Music*, the real Maria was no flighty cloud that needed pinning down but a stalwart and intelligent convert to Catholicism who wrote several books, one of which contains her family's Austrian customs for the liturgical year.

CHRISTMAS PUNCH

1 sliced pineapple
1 bottle claret (or any hearty, dry red wine)
1 bottle red wine
½ bottle rum
juice of 4 lemons
juice of 4 oranges
1 pint water
1 lb. sugar
grated rind of 1 lemon
grated rind of 1 orange
4 whole oranges cut in pieces
1 stick cinnamon, broken up
1 vanilla bean
½ cup maraschino cherries
champagne

Boil spices thoroughly with the water. Remove them and pour the water into large earthenware pot. Add lemon and orange and rind, as well as pineapple and sugar (fruit and sugar prepared in a separate dish). Then add wine and rum; cover and heat. Add champagne before serving.

Maria does not stipulate how many this will serve, but we would wager that it provides around two dozen servings.

CHRISTMAS PUNCH FOR CHILDREN

1 qt. grape juice   juice of 2 lemons
2 qts. water   juice of 2 oranges
2 cups sugar   rind of above lemons and
½ tsp. whole cloves   oranges
1 stick cinnamon

Boil sugar, water, lemon rind, and spices until flavored. Mix with the rest of the ingredients, boil five minutes, and serve hot in punch glasses.

BEER AND WINE

There are well over two hundred ales, beers, or porters with the word "Christmas," "Noël," "Navidad," or "Weinacht" on their label. Let local availability be your guide.

Domaine de Martinolles is a winery that keeps alive the traditions and vineyards begun by the monks of the Benedictine Abbey of St. Hilaire in Saint-Hilaire, France in 1531. The winery makes a number of still and sparkling wines such as their Brut Le Berceau, which is French for "The Cradle"—presumably, the cradle of Our Lord. Enjoy some bubbly tonight, either on its own or in a champagne cocktail (or in the Von Trapps' Christmas punch).

LAST CALL

The word "wassail" comes from the Old Saxon toast, *Was haile*—Your health! Tonight and throughout the Twelve Days of Christmas, use this ancient drinker's greeting, along with a traditional Christmas greeting borrowed from the Byzantine rite. One person proclaims, "Christ is born!" and the other replies, "Glorify Him!"

ST. STEPHEN, DECEMBER 26

St. Stephen, one of the first seven men ordained a deacon by the guidance of the Holy Spirit, is called the protomartyr, for in being stoned to death by order of the Sanhedrin, he was the first disciple of Christ to shed his blood for the Faith (Acts 6:5-7:59). Stephen is a model of that divinely-infused love known in the Christian tradition as *agape* or *caritas*, the gift of God which in English we call "charity." Charity's divine origin cannot be overemphasized, for it is by no human love that someone can follow the example of our Savior and forgive the men

murdering him. Yet as St. Luke tells us, as Stephen was dying he fell to his knees and cried out in a loud voice: "Lord, lay not this sin to their charge."

By a strange twist of history, St. Stephen is also the patron saint of horses, so feel free tonight to make good use of any Kentucky bourbon in a nod to the nation's most famous horse race, the Derby.

You can also have something a little more directly connected to our saint, such as a cocktail sharing the protomartyr's name. The oh-so-Catholic Bénédictine liqueur is a nice touch.

STEPHEN'S COCKTAIL

1 oz. sherry   ¾ oz. Bénédictine
¾ oz. dry vermouth

Pour ingredients into an old-fashioned glass filled with ice and stir.

Or, in honor of one of the Church's first seven members of the diaconate, have a Rosy Deacon or a Pale Deacon. Sloe gin is a delicious liqueur made from sloeberry, aka blackthorn plum.

ROSY DEACON

¾ oz. gin   1 oz. grapefruit juice
¾ oz. sloe gin   sugar to taste

Pour all ingredients into a shaker filled with ice and shake forty times. Strain into a cocktail glass.

PALE DEACON

1¼ oz. gin   ½ tsp. sugar
1¼ oz. grapefruit juice

Pour all ingredients into a shaker filled with ice and shake forty times. Strain into a cocktail glass.

Lastly, see if you can track down a bottle of Saint Etienne Rum from Martinique, bottled by Habitation Saint Etienne.

BEER AND WINE

The Selkirk Abbey Brewing Company in northern Idaho makes a St. Stephen Saison, the Mystery Brewing Company in Hillsborough, North Carolina makes a St. Stephen's Green (a dry Irish stout), and the Belgian

Brouwerij Van Steenberge has a number of St. Stefanus brews, named after the Augustinian monastery of St. Stefanus in Ghent. Failing all these options, go shopping for any beer with a horse on the label.

For a French wine, look for any bottle with the appellation Saint-Estèphe, one of the AOCs for red wine in the region of Bordeaux in the Médoc sub region. Or look to the Côtes du Rhône and to the winery Château St-Estève at Uchaux. Estèphe and Estève, incidentally, are corruptions of Etienne, the French word for Stephen.

In Italy, the Santo Stefano vineyard produces some of the Piemonte region's best grapes that are used by wineries such as Castello di Neive. There is also a Santo Stefano winery in California's Napa Valley.

LAST CALL

Stephen's is the traditional day on which the abundance of Christmas is shared with the less fortunate. It was on this day that the poor boxes of the church were emptied and their contents distributed to the needy—hence the term "Boxing Day." Today, do something nice for the poor, like giving a homeless person some food or warm clothes. Then, say a prayer for the less fortunate before wassailing in gratitude for the blessings God has given you.

ST. JOHN THE EVANGELIST, DECEMBER 27

Like St. Stephen, St. John the Apostle and Evangelist is associated with charity, since his writings marvelously emphasize the love of God (see John 3:16, I John 4:7-8). John, in turn, was blessed by Christ's special love for him. Although our Lord made St. Peter the head of His Church, He retained a personal affection for the "beloved disciple." This is all the more endearing given the fact that Our Lord also referred to John and his older brother St. James the Great as "sons of thunder," most likely for their fiery tempers (Mk. 3:17).

It has been said that St. John was the only Apostle who did not die a martyr's death because he had already testified to the Cross by being the only apostle who stood at its foot with the Mother of God. Yet the Church still honors John as a martyr because several attempts on his life were made. Perhaps the saint's most famous brush with death was when his enemies tried to kill him by poisoning his cup of wine. Some say that when the Divine John (as he is called in the East) made the sign of the cross over the cup, it split in half. Others claim that his blessing neutralized the poison in the potation and allowed him to enjoy it unharmed. Either way, it is a good reminder to say one's grace before meals.

And it is also the inspiration for consuming the "Love of St. John" (*Johannesminne* or *Szent Janos Aldasa*), wine or cider that is blessed by the priest after Mass with a special blessing from the Roman Ritual and poured into everyone's glass before dinner later that night. The blessed liquid was considered a sacramental and used in a variety of ways: it was poured into every barrel of the family wine cellar or kept in the house throughout the year for newlyweds to drink immediately after the wedding ceremony, for travelers before a trip, and for the dying after receiving Last Rites as "the last earthly drink to strengthen them for their departure from this world." *

St. John's Wine can also be mulled for a spicy hot drink on a cold winter's night. Here is a recipe from William Kaufman's *Catholic Cookbook* that makes an ideal treat for the entire family, since most of the alcohol is evaporated in the process.

ST. JOHN'S WINE

1 quart red wine	2 two-inch cinnamon sticks
½ cup sugar	½ tsp. ground nutmeg
3 whole cloves	1/16 tsp. ground cardamom

Pour all the ingredients into a large saucepan and boil for five minutes. Serve hot. Makes approximately eight one-cup servings.

---

* Francis X. Weiser, *Handbook of Christian Feasts and Customs* (Harcourt, Brace, & World, 1958), 130.

Of course, since the blessing on St. John's Day mentions wine "or any other drink," why not enjoy your favorite whiskey? Or, have one of two mixed drinks in honor of the Beloved Disciple, the first of which, to our way of thinking, commemorates his nickname "Son of Thunder."

THUNDERCLAP

¾ oz. gin   1 oz. brandy
¾ oz. rye or bourbon

Pour all ingredients in a mixing glass with ice and stir forty times. Strain into a cocktail glass.

Or try an invention from Fr. John Grant and his comrades who kept a "Saints and Spirits" tradition while they were seminarians. A "James and John on the Rocks" honors the two Sons of Thunder who, as brothers, also get to share a drink. And isn't the Rock St. Peter, with whom they were in union?

JAMES AND JOHN ON THE ROCKS

By the "Saints and Spirits" band of brothers at St. John
   Vianney Seminary in Denver, Colorado
1 oz. Jameson Irish whiskey   1 oz. Johnny Walker scotch

Mix ingredients into an old-fashioned glass filled with ice and stir.

It is eminently desirable to have St. John's Love blessed by a priest after today's Mass, since a sacerdotal blessing has a special efficacy. However, since it behooves every layman to bless his family and his food or drink, one should not fail to pray this blessing tonight even if you are bereft of Holy Orders.

> O Lord God, deign to bless and consecrate with Thy right hand this cup of wine and of any drink whatsoever: and grant that by the merits of Saint John the Apostle and Evangelist all who believe in Thee and who drink from this cup may be blessed and protected.

LAST CALL

Our Christmas guide Maria Von Trapp describes the Austrian ceremony involving St. John's Love. Before the dinner, everyone stands up with his glass of blessed wine. The father then takes his glass, touches it to the mother's while looking her in the eyes and says, "I drink to you the love of St. John," to which the mother replies, "I thank you for the love of St. John." Both take a sip before the mother turns to the oldest child and repeats the ritual, at which point the child turns to the next oldest, etc. The last one to receive St. John's love (the youngest member of the family) gives it back to the father, thus closing the family circle.

And as Blessed John drank poison from a cup and remained completely unharmed, may all who drink from this cup on this day in honor of Blessed John be, by his merits, rescued from every sickness of poison and from every kind of harm; and, offering themselves up body and soul, may they be delivered from all fault. Through Christ our Lord. Amen.

Bless, O Lord, this drink, Thy creation: that it may be a salutary remedy for all who consume it: and grant through the invocation of Thy holy name that whoever tastes of it may, by Thy generosity, receive health of the soul as well as of the body. Through Christ our Lord. Amen.

And may the blessing of almighty God, Father, Son, and Holy Ghost, descend upon this wine, Thy creation, and upon any drink whatsoever, and remain forever. Amen.

HOLY INNOCENTS, DECEMBER 28

Herod, perceiving that he was deluded by the wise men, was exceeding angry; and sending killed all the men children that were in Bethlehem, and in all the borders thereof, from two years old and under, according to the time which he had diligently inquired of the wise men (Mt. 2:16-17).

From what we can tell, the Roman rite has always kept the feast of "Childermas" (Children's Mass) on December 28, ever since it first began being celebrated in the fifth century. In so doing, the Western Church presents an interesting array of saints on December 26, 27, and 28. Stephen is a martyr by will, love, and blood; John the Evangelist a martyr by will and love (but not blood because he died a natural death); and the Holy Innocents are martyrs by blood alone. Indeed, because these children died not only for Christ but instead of Him they are called *flores martyrum*, the "flowers of the martyrs." As St. Augustine eloquently puts it: "They are the first buds of the Church killed by the frost of persecution."

Tonight, exercise your imagination and have any floral-themed libation. It could be a drink with a floral name or something with a floral ingredient, such as the elderflower in St. Germain liqueur or a cocktail with passionflower syrup.

Or, honor the childer in Childermas with a Kiddie Car Cocktail. You can use the apple brandy left over from Christmas Eve.

KIDDIE CAR

1¾ oz. apple brandy   ¼ oz. triple sec
½ oz. fresh lime juice

Pour all ingredients into a shaker filled with ice forty times and shake forty times. Strain into a cocktail glass.

LAST CALL

As we mentioned earlier, the Twelve Days of Christmas are a time of "topsy-turvy" customs, where social ranks and pecking orders are inverted in giddy imitation of the grandest inversion of all, the fact that Almighty God humbled Himself to be born a man in a chilly and malodorous stable. Childermas is no exception. In many religious communities, the novices had the privilege of sitting at the head of the table at meals and meetings, while the last person who had taken vows in the monastery or convent got to be superior for a day. Young monks and nuns would receive congratulations and have "baby food," such as hot cereal, served to them for dinner. In the family, the youngest child received special honors, even becoming master of the household. Not all customs, however, bode well for the young 'uns. In some places, children awoke to a spanking from their parents to remind them of the sufferings of the Holy Innocents!

In the Philippines and some Spanish-speaking countries, Childermas is the equivalent of April Fools' Day, a time of pranks and practical jokes called *inocentadas*. And, of course, all of Christendom once abstained from servile work on this day—along with the other twelve days of Christmas.

Today, come up with your own topsy-turvy, prankish, leisurely customs. A good snort might help with the creative process.

ST. THOMAS BECKET, DECEMBER 29

Thomas Becket (ca. 1118–1170) became Archbishop of Canterbury in 1162 and soon began defending the rights of the Church against the encroachment of his former friend King Henry II. The most galvanizing issue was whether English clergymen were under the jurisdiction of ecclesiastical courts or the king's. Becket refused to budge, and eventually the exacerbated king was overheard by some of his knights to say, "Will no one rid me of this meddlesome priest?" Four of them took his words to heart, marched off to Canterbury, and slew Becket in his cathedral as he was approaching the sanctuary for Solemn Vespers on December 29.* Thus, as a hymn in his honor puts it, St. Thomas became "both priest and sacrifice in the church of Canterbury for the sake of the laws of justice."

Normally if a saint's heavenly birthday falls within the octave of Christmas it is transferred to another date, but the faithful were so shocked that a bishop during the

---

* The four knights were subsequently excommunicated and were readmitted into the Church on condition that they serve fourteen years in the Crusades, a veritable death sentence.

height of Christendom would be martyred by a Christian king that Becket's feast day was allowed to remain on the anniversary of his martyrdom. Tonight, toast Becket with your favorite English ale or beer. Or, have a barely original cocktail called Becket's Well. The name is taken from a legend about Becket as he traveled through Otford, Kent. The saint did not like the taste of the drinking water and struck his crosier on the ground to form what became known as Becket's Well. The drink itself is a variation of the Fare Thee Well cocktail.

BECKET'S WELL

1½ oz. gin	¼ oz. sweet vermouth
¼ oz. dry vermouth	¼ oz. orange curaçao

Stir ingredients in a mixing glass with ice forty times and strain into a cocktail glass.

Or, since 'tis the season for punches, make an Archbishop Punch tonight. True, it doesn't come in a large bowl, but it does fulfill the original meaning of "punch," which is a drink with five ingredients (usually alcohol, water, lemon, sugar, and tea or spices). The addition of Jamaican rum in 1655 is what makes the Archbishop a modern punch as opposed to a wine or brandy-based wassail (p. 108).

ARCHBISHOP PUNCH

2 oz. port
2 oz. water
1 oz. fresh lime juice

½ tsp. sugar
½ oz. Jamaican rum

Build ingredients in a highball glass filled with ice.

LAST CALL

Our favorite legend about St. Thomas Becket is the following. Once, a little bird that had been taught to speak escaped from its cage and flew into a field. A hawk swooped in for the kill, and as it was about to strike, the panicked bird cried out what it had heard others say in times of distress, "Saint Thomas, help!" The hawk was struck dead, and the bird escaped unharmed. Tonight, raise your glass, and in imitation of the smart little critter say, "St. Thomas, help!"

ST. JUCUNDUS OF AOSTA, DECEMBER 30

We don't know a great deal about St. Jucundus, except that he lived in the early sixth century, was a bishop of Aosta, Italy, and participated in synods at Rome in 501 and 502. He is sometimes confused with another St. Jucundus who was martyred in Rheims, France, and was later anachronistically portrayed as a companion of Saint Gratus of Aosta (d. 470). And as if this weren't enough, there are half a dozen other early saints named Jucundus.

But we do know two things: 1) Jucundus's name means "merry," "joyful," or "jocund" and, 2) there is a San Giocondo wine (his name in Italian) produced by the Santa Cristina estate of the Antinori winery. Put these two things together, and it can only mean that we should grow joyful with his wine. We're sure he would have wanted it that way, whoever he was.

Or, honor "Saint Merry" with a Merry Go Round cocktail, as we all go round and round about which St. Jucundus was which.

MERRY GO ROUND

1½ oz. gin
½ oz. sweet vermouth
½ oz. dry vermouth

1 olive and 1 lemon twist for garnish

Pour all ingredients except lemon and olive into a shaker filled with ice and shake forty times. Strain into a cocktail glass and garnish with lemon twist and olive.

ST. FELIX, MAY 30 (DECEMBER 30)

Providence has a wry sense of humor, assigning not one but two saints to December 30 who: 1) have a jovial name and 2) are confused with other saints who have the same jovial name. St. Felix I, which means "happy" or "lucky," was a pope who ruled the Church from 269 to 274. He is often confused with a martyr who died around the same time, and in the traditional calendar his feast day was assigned to May 30 instead of the day he died (December 30) because a scribe way-back-when had written "III Kal. Jun." (third day to the calends of *June*) instead of "III Kal. Jan." (third day to the calends of *January*). Obviously, Our Lord really wants both Jucundus and Felix to be remembered on the same day within the Octave of His birthday so we can say both "Merry Christmas" and "Happy Christmas," and both with a double meaning.

For Pope Felix, the happy head of the Church, have a Jolly Pilot.

JOLLY PILOT

By Edith Carlile

1½ oz. gin
½ oz. Amontillado sherry
½ oz. Cointreau
½ oz. brandy

1 dash Angostura bitters
1 lemon twist and 1 pearl
    onion for garnish (optional)

Pour all ingredients except lemon and onion into a shaker filled with ice and shake forty times. Strain into a cocktail glass and garnish with lemon twist and onion.

BEER AND WINE

The craft brewery Grado Plato in Chieri, Italy, makes a chestnut amber Strada San Felice (named after an old street). But it will probably be easier to track down a bottle of San Felice. The winery operates in several parts of Tuscany, including its famed Chianti Classic DOC region.

ST. SYLVESTER, DECEMBER 31

 St. Sylvester was Supreme Pontiff during the reign of Constantine, the Roman Emperor who ended the persecution of the Church. One legend even claims that Sylvester baptized Constantine after the latter was miraculously cured from leprosy.

There is a simple reason why the saint's feast falls on this day: after twenty-one years of service to God as pope, Sylvester died and was buried on December 31, 335. That said, there is something appropriate about preparing for the new civic year with the first Bishop of Rome to assume the throne of Peter during a time of civic peace, since this is the time when our hearts are filled with hope for "peace on earth." Sylvester's feast is so closely tied to December 31 that in many countries New Year's Eve is known as Sylvester Night (*Silvesterabend* or *Silvesternacht* in German).

The now-defunct Sansilvestro was a proprietary herbal liqueur made with suspended flakes of silver. Putting flakes of precious metals into drinks, which goes back to ancient times, makes no change to the flavor and poses no risks to the body. Indeed, some folks claim that it aids the circulation and acts as an antioxidant.

As a nod to the old Sansilvestro liqueur and as a memorable way of wishing prosperity on you and your guests on New Year's Eve, let's drink some gold. See below for our champagne suggestions. As for the stronger stuff, Vinos y Licores Azteca and El Cartel distilleries have tequilas with gold or silver flakes, and there are several Europeans liqueurs with gold such as Liqueur D'Or and Goldwasser (p. 175), but probably the easiest option to find in the U.S. is a cinnamon schnapps with gold flakes by a company such as Goldschläger or Grand Royale. "Gold in Harlem" is the name of a lovely champagne cocktail invented by Amy Wisniewski that includes Goldschläger schnapps (see CHOW.com). It was the inspiration for our own "Godly Prosperity" cocktail, which was perfected with the help of our friends Logan and Liz Gage. Appropriately, the name comes from a New Year's wish by St. Thomas More to a friend.

Finally, let the faithful Catholics of Poland adorn the night with a potent *Poncz Sylwestrowy*, or the faithful Catholics of Germany with a visually marvelous and tasty Fire Punch (*Feuerzangenbowle*).

GODLY PROSPERITY

½ oz. cinnamon schnapps
   with gold flakes
¼ oz. fresh lemon juice

3 oz. chilled brut sparkling
   wine
1 dash orange bitters
cranberry garnish

Build ingredients in a champagne coupe or saucer glass. (You can also use a champagne flute, but it won't show the gold flakes as well.) Throw in a cranberry for some holiday color, but don't eat it unless you like extreme tartness.

Sylvester Punches are a traditional way in Catholic cultures to usher in the new year. Here are two recipes for the occasion from Maria Von Trapp. The second is an alcohol-free version for the little ones which we have taken the liberty of naming Maria's Punchless Punch.

MARIA VON TRAPP'S SYLVESTER PUNCH
(APPROXIMATELY TWELVE ONE-CUP SERVINGS)

1 750 ml bottle of red
  burgundy
750 ml hot tea
12 cloves

rind of 1 lemon, thinly pared
2 tbsp. sugar
2 cinnamon sticks

Pour the wine into a pot and add cloves, lemon, sugar, and cinnamon. Heat over a low flame but do not allow to boil. At the last moment add the tea. Serve hot.

MARIA'S PUNCHLESS PUNCH

½ cup fresh lemon juice
rind of 1 lemon, grated
1 qt. water

1 cup orange juice
1 cup sugar
grated rind of ½ orange

Cook sugar and water for five minutes. Cool. Add juices and rind.

.The Von Trapp family also created a little variety each year by adding one of the following to the basic recipe: 1) 1 cup grated pineapple and 1 qt. ginger ale; 2) 1 qt. strained and sweetened strawberry juice, 1 qt. raspberry juice, and 2 qts. ginger ale; 3) 1 glass currant jelly dissolved in 1 cup hot water (cooked and then chilled) and ¼ cup finely minced mint; and 4) 1 qt. cider, 1 qt. grape juice, and 1 qt. soda water.

One suggestion: Our panel of junior tasters found the punch a bit too sweet. Rather than pour in the entire cup of sugar, you may wish to add to taste.

Finally, here is a "delicious (and potent) punch from Poland" made with white wine and rum. The recipe serves approximately sixteen half-cup servings.

PONCZ SYLWESTROWY*

2 oranges	4 cups white wine
2 lemons	2 cups light rum
sugar to taste (about 1 cup)	

Juice the oranges and lemons and grate the orange and lemon rinds. Combine the rind with sugar, wine, and rum in a large pan. Add the juices of the orange and lemon. Heat but do not boil. Serve hot. Note: If the punch is too strong or sweet, it can be diluted with hot water. At our last Silvesternacht, we added one cup of water and liked it better.

---

* From Evelyn Vitz, *A Continual Feast* (Ignatius Press, 1985), 159.

FEUERZANGENBOWLE (FIRE PUNCH)

151-proof rum
  (approximately 1 to 2 cups)
sugar cone
2 bottles Merlot
1 cup orange juice (pulp-free)

½ cup fresh lemon juice
8 orange slices
8 lemon slices
4 cinnamon sticks
10 whole cloves

In a large stainless pot combine everything but the sugar cone and the rum. Heat the mixture over medium heat until hot, but not boiling. Pour the hot mixture into a heatproof glass punch-bowl set.* Light the candle below the punchbowl to keep the mixture warm.

Place the stainless steel "bridge" across the glass punch-bowl and place the sugar cone on top. Carefully pour the 151-proof rum over the sugar cone, rotating the cone to make sure the whole cone absorbs the rum.

Immediately turn the lights down low, gather your guests around and use a long gas lighter or long match to carefully set the cone on fire. Allow the flame to melt the sugar, which will slowly drip into the wine making a show for your guests and filling the room with aromatic scents of the holidays.

Serve the hot punch in a heat-proof clear glass with a handle. You may garnish each glass with an orange and/or lemon slice and a cinnamon stick if you wish.

---

* The heatproof glass punchbowl, stainless steel bridge, and sugar cone are available through online retailers such as GermanDeli.com.

LAST CALL

Sylvester Night traditionally abounds with charming customs. In France and French Canada it was customary for the father to bless the members of his family and for the children to thank their parents for all of their love and care. In central Europe, a pre-Christian ritual of scaring away demons with loud noises became the inspiration for our New Year's Eve custom of fireworks and artillery salutes. In Austria, December 31 was sometimes called *Rauhnacht* or "Incense night," when the paterfamilias went through the house and barn purifying them with incense and holy water. In Spain and other Spanish-speaking areas it was considered good luck to eat twelve grapes at the twelve strokes of midnight.

Holy Mother Church also grants a plenary indulgence, under the usual conditions, to a public recitation of the great Latin hymn of thanksgiving, the *Te Deum*, on the last day of the year, while a partial indulgence "is granted to those who recite the *Te Deum* in thanksgiving." Sing or say the *Te Deum* tonight, or if you lack the time, at least make a toast filled with thanksgiving for the previous year.

Lastly, paraphrase St. Thomas More and wish each of your guests a year of "godly prosperity," a year that sees a "happy continuation and gracious increase of virtue" in their souls.

BEER AND WINE

The Brasserie de Saint-Sylvestre in French Flanders produces a number of well-regarded beers, some of which are exported to the U.S.

For sparkling wine containing flakes of real gold, look for Blue Nun 24k Gold Edition or a bottle of Jade Or de Malidain from the Loire Valley in France. As for honoring St. Sylvester's name, Cantine San Silvestro in Italy produces some of the leading DOC and DOCG red wines in the celebrated region of Piemonte or Piedmont.

FEAST OF THE CIRCUMCISION/ MARY, MOTHER OF GOD, JANUARY 1

Over the centuries, January 1 in the calendar of the Latin Church came to be a combination of three feasts: the Octave Day of Christmas, the Maternity of the Blessed Virgin Mary, and the Feast of the Circumcision of Our Lord—which, according to the Gospel, took place on the octave of His birth (Lk. 2:21). In the post-Vatican II calendar, January 1 is known as the Octave of the Nativity and the Solemnity of Mary, Mother of God.

"Bad Catholic" John Zmirak impishly offers Bloody Marys as a tie-in to the Feast of the Circumcision,* but there is another reason to heed his suggestion. Most drinking on New Year's Day, if it takes place at all, takes place during brunch, and the Bloody Mary is an ideal brunch drink. Plus, one way to "translate" the phrase Bloody

---

* *The Bad Catholic's Guide to Good Living* (Crossroad, 2005), 214.

Mary is "By our Lady, Mary", thereby hearkening to the Marian dimension of the day.

BLOODY MARY

1½ oz. vodka
3 oz. tomato juice
1 dash fresh lemon juice
½ tsp. Worcestershire sauce
2 or 3 drops Tabasco hot sauce

salt and pepper
lemon or lime wedge, celery
  stick, or olives for garnish
  (optional)

Place all ingredients except garnishes in a shaker filled with ice and shake forty times. Strain into an old-fashioned or highball glass filled with ice. Garnish.

BEER

Emmanuales (see p. 99) has a spiced barley wine called Ale Mary. They describe it thus: "Made using festive spices, and once likened to 'drinking a mince pie,' this dark ruby ale is a whole heap of Christmas in a glass. So turn that Cliff Richard up to eleven and drink to the King!"

LAST CALL

Holy Mother Church grants a plenary indulgence when the great hymn to the Holy Spirit, *Veni Creator Spiritus* or "Come Holy Ghost, Creator Blest," is recited on January 1 under the usual conditions. Belt it out today with gusto; even if you don't meet the requirements for a plenary indulgence, you can still start the year off right with a Bloody Mary and a partial indulgence.

FEAST OF THE HOLY NAME OF JESUS, JANUARY 2 (JANUARY 3)

January 1 was the day that Our Lord was formally given the name Jesus, on the occasion of His circumcision (Lk. 2:21). But since January 1 is already somewhat crowded with things to celebrate, it makes sense that the Church would reserve a special day to honor Our Lord's saving name. In the 1962 calendar, that day is the Sunday between January 1 and 6 or otherwise on January 2; in the new Church calendar, it is January 3, put there by Pope St. John Paul II after the feast had been dropped from the 1970 calendar.

The Holy Name of Jesus, foretold to both St. Joseph and the Blessed Virgin Mary months before His birth, means "Yahweh Saves." To honor the Savior God who loves us so much that He came into the world on Christmas Day, try the following:

HE LOVES ME

1 oz. gin
½ oz. sweet vermouth
¼ oz. grenadine
¼ oz. pineapple juice

1 egg white
1 pineapple spear for
    garnish

Pour all ingredients except the pineapple spear into a shaker filled with ice and shake forty times. Strain into a cocktail glass and garnish with pineapple.

St. Genevieve

Genevieve (419/422–512) was a girl when St. Germanus of Auxerre and St. Lupus of Troyes stopped at her hometown of Nanterre in France to preach. St. Germanus saw in her a sign of great holiness and told her parents so. Genevieve later moved to Paris and became a nun. When the city was threatened by Attila the Hun, her prayers helped turn him away; even centuries after her death, a procession of her relics through the streets of Paris averted a deadly epidemic of ergot poisoning.

Since St. Genevieve is the patroness of the City of Light, mix yourself a delightfully flavorful Paris cocktail.

Paris Cocktail

¾ oz. gin
¾ oz. Grand Marnier

½ oz. cherry liqueur (Cherry Heering, etc.)
½ oz. fresh lemon juice

Pour ingredients into shaker filled with ice and shake forty times. Strain into a cocktail glass.

WINE

In the saint's homeland, Domaine de Vignes du Maynes in Burgundy makes a well-regarded Ste. Geneviève sparkling wine in white and rosé. In the U.S., Sainte Genevieve Winery is a family-owned business in Sainte Genevieve, Missouri (the oldest French settlement west of the Mississippi) that makes quality wine in small lots. The Ste. Genevieve Wines of Fort Stockton, Texas, on the other hand, will probably be a more accessible alternative. Ste. Genevieve is the largest of Texas' 588 wineries and has received a number of awards on the state, national, and international levels.

LAST CALL

To St. Genevieve: may she protect us from today's barbarians.

ST. ELIZABETH ANN SETON, JANUARY 4

St. Elizabeth Ann Seton (1774–1821) came from a prominent New York Episcopalian family and married the import trader William Magee Seton at the age of nineteen. William suffered bankruptcy and then contracted tuberculosis; he and Elizabeth visited Italy and its warmer climes at the advice of his doctors, but William died not long after reaching their destination. It was William's Italian business partners who introduced Elizabeth to Catholicism, and upon her return to the United States she converted. She was received into the Church at St. Peter's in New York, the only Catholic church in the city at the time, and was later confirmed by the Right Reverend John Carroll, the only bishop in the nation. Elizabeth tried to start an academy for young ladies, but parents withdrew their children from it when they discovered she was Catholic. Eventually she founded a Catholic school for the poor in Baltimore and in this way began the Catholic parochial school system; she also established a religious community called the Sisters of Charity in Emmitsburg, Maryland. St. Elizabeth died of tuberculosis at the age of forty-six.

We like Mother Seton a lot, but we couldn't help but notice that her family and her husband's family as well were British loyalists during the Revolutionary War. With a nod to this history—and in the hopes that St. Elizabeth has a sense of humor—we honor her today with a cocktail known as the Benedict Arnold. At least the Bénédictine liqueur is Catholic.

BENEDICT ARNOLD

1½ oz. scotch   ½ oz. Bénédictine liqueur

Pour into an old-fashioned glass with ice and stir until cold.

Another option, in keeping with the Twelve Days of Christmas, is to have a punch or mulled wine mixed with the liqueur St. Elizabeth Allspice Dram. St. Elizabeth is a rum flavored with allspice, a complex berry that already has hints of Christmastime spices such as clove, cinnamon, and nutmeg. If one of your guests points out that this liqueur is probably not named after today's Saint Elizabeth, glare at him and take away his drink.

TWELFTH NIGHT, JANUARY 5

January 5 is the twelfth day of Christmas, and hence the evening of January 5 is known as Twelfth Night. Exploiting a precedent set by the Roman Saturnalia, the Twelve Days of Christmas are a joyful imitation of the ultimate role reversal, when almighty God became a helpless infant in order to become our suffering servant. Topsy-turvy customs were common during the Twelve Days, such as servants dressing as masters and men and women cross-dressing. This was especially true during the grand finale of the Christmas celebrations, Twelfth Night. Shakespeare's play by that name, believed to have been written as a Christmastime entertainment, gives many a nod to these gender-bending customs.

Tonight, enjoy any of the drinks of the Epiphany (p. 174) on this its vigil, but do so while decked in the raiment of the opposite sex.

WINE AND BEER

Vela Wines in Central Otago, New Zealand has a Twelfth Night label of wines that varies annually. Past years include Pinot Noir, Riesling, Sauvignon Blanc, and Gewürztraminer. Twelfth Night wines are currently available in Connecticut, Florida, Maryland, Massachusetts, New Hampshire, New York, Pennsylvania, Virginia, and Washington, D.C.

Lickinghole Creek Craft Brewery in Virginia makes a big (11.2% ABV) Twelfth Night Belgian-Style Quad Ale that looks quite promising but has limited distribution.

"THE TWELVE DAYS OF CHRISTMAS" THE SONG

ALSO FROM DECEMBER 25 TO JANUARY 5

I n the previous chapter we explained the Twelve Days of Christmas and offered drink suggestions based on the Church calendar. In this chapter, we pair drink suggestions with the familiar Christmas carol "The Twelve Days of Christmas." Feel free to flip back and forth between the two in order to find the drink that better suits your needs.

It may seem odd to include a secular song like "The Twelve Days of Christmas" in a pious bartender's guide, but there *could* be a Catholic connection. According to one theory, the carol was invented by English recusant Catholics as an esoteric catechism to pass the Faith down to their children during the dark days of Elizabethan persecution, with each gift from "my true love" (God) representing an article of belief. Historians tend to reject this theory, but we find it useful in firing up the Catholic allegorical imagination in young and old alike during Christmastime. Besides: since when does a drinking occasion need to be based on solid scholarship?

In this chapter, then, we present each verse of "The Twelve Days of Christmas" followed by a theological interpretation and an appropriate beverage. But one note of caution before we begin: For the sake of your liver and your family, do *not* follow the conventions of the song and drink cumulatively.

So, take a breath and bellow out: "On the first day of Christmas, my true love gave to me…"

DECEMBER 25—
"ON THE FIRST DAY OF CHRISTMAS, MY TRUE LOVE GAVE TO ME A PARTRIDGE IN A PEAR TREE"

The partridge in a pear tree represents Jesus Christ. Like a mother partridge that protects her young by feigning injury and drawing the predator to herself, Jesus takes our sins upon Himself and dies for us. The pear tree signifies either the wood of the manger or of the cross while the fruit from the tree reminds us of the Fall of Adam and Eve that led to our Lord becoming the New Adam, that He might deliver us from the evil unleashed by our first parents' foolish fruit binge.

Chilled pear liqueur is a good after-dinner choice: Poire William is a well-regarded French pear liqueur, and several producers, believe it or not, have an entire pear inside each bottle. A bottle is placed around a small pear bud on the tree, and the pear grows up inside it.

Another option is a delicious Partridge in a Pear Tree Cocktail. The original recipe calls for only one ounce of gin and is perfect for those people who don't like the taste of alcohol in their drinks, but we thought it could use a little more of a kick. And, of course, the rosemary is a part of traditional Christmas lore (see p. 178).

Partridge in a Pear Tree Cocktail

By Julie Hartigan

4 oz. pear nectar
1-1½ oz. gin
½ oz. fresh lemon juice
½ oz. rosemary simple
 syrup

sliced pear and fresh
 rosemary sprigs for
 garnish

Pour all liquid ingredients into a shaker filled with ice and shake forty times. Strain into an old-fashioned glass and garnish with a slice of pear and small sprig of rosemary. To make rosemary simple syrup, use the following easy recipe.

Note: Pear nectar can be surprisingly difficult to find. Guava nectar (a relative of the pear) makes a good substitute. We won't tell the partridge if you don't.

Rosemary Simple Syrup (Yields enough for 24 cocktails)

1 cup water
1 cup sugar

4 large sprigs of rosemary

Boil and stir equal water and sugar with rosemary sprigs until the sugar is dissolved and then let cool. Remove the rosemary by straining it.

Note: You can also cheat by muddling or crushing rosemary sprigs into a regular simple syrup.

CIDER AND BEER

For the partridge's favorite hangout, how about some pear cider? Ace, Angry Orchard, Argus Cidery, Crispin, Magners, Rekorderlig, Woodchuck, and Wyder are among the brands that produce a pear cider. Many of these have a similar profile as champagne and pair nicely with fruits, cheeses, and salads.

Unibroue brewery in Chambly, Quebec produces seasonal beers under their Éphémères label. One of them is Éphémère Poire, a white ale brewed with pears.

LAST CALL

A toast: "A most happy birthday to our true love, Jesus Christ, who deigned to be born this day to take the Devil off our scent. Merry Christmas."

DECEMBER 26—
"ON THE SECOND DAY OF CHRISTMAS, MY TRUE LOVE GAVE TO ME TWO TURTLE DOVES"

Two turtle doves represent the two principal parts of the Bible, the Old and New Testament. Like turtle doves, which mate for life, there is a profound and indivisible affinity between the two Testaments. And the dove is a symbol of the Holy Spirit, who inspired the composition of both Testaments. Finally, turtle doves obviously remind us of the Christmas story, when Joseph and Mary offered up a pair of these birds in accordance with the Old Law as they presented Jesus in the Temple (Luke 2:23-24).

Tonight, make yourself a Turtle Dove Martini or a Chocolate Turtle Martini. Oh wait; the song says *two* turtle doves. Better make it both.

TURTLE DOVE MARTINI

Adapted by askannamoseley.com

2 oz. vanilla vodka	1½ oz. whole milk
2 oz. Frangelico	nutmeg for garnish
1 oz. amaretto	

Pour all ingredients except nutmeg into a shaker filled with ice and shake forty times. Strain into a cocktail glass and sprinkle with nutmeg. The nutmeg gives the drink a speckled look, much like the back of a turtle dove. And FYI, the drink also works well without the milk.

CHOCOLATE TURTLE MARTINI

By Dove Chocolate Discoveries

1 oz. DCD Chocolate Martini Mix	1 cup crushed ice
1 oz. vanilla vodka	DCD Chef-Series Chocolate (for garnish)
1 oz. pecan-flavored liqueur	Toasted pecans (for garnish)

Rim a cocktail glass with DCD chocolate by dipping it in melted chocolate. Pour all liquid ingredients and crushed ice into the glass and garnish with pecans.

WINE AND BEER

There is a Whispering Dove Vineyards in Napa Valley, but its bottlings may be harder to catch than two turtle doves in a bush; the same goes for St. Clement Vineyards' Ark and Dove Red Blend, also from Napa.

Depending on where you live, you may have similar luck tracking down one of the several beers with a connection to doves, such as the products of Naked Dove Brewing Company, Dove Mountain Brewing Company, and Little Dove New World-style pale ale by Gage Roads Brewing Company.

LAST CALL

Amaze (or bore) your friends by asking them to guess where the turtle dove got its name. After they run out of jokes about flying shelled creatures, take a dramatic swig of your drink and explain that the name is onomatopoeic for the vibrating "turrr, turrr" of their song. Then, raise your glass and offer the following toast: "To the turtle dove: may we be as faithful to our vows—baptismal, marital, or religious—as they are to each other."

DECEMBER 27—
"ON THE THIRD DAY OF CHRISTMAS, MY TRUE LOVE GAVE TO ME THREE FRENCH HENS"

The three French hens could stand for the three Divine Persons in the Holy Trinity or the three gifts of the Magi, but the more common interpretation is that they are the three theological virtues of faith, hope, and charity, poured fourth into our hearts by the Holy Spirit.

Why are Englishmen singing about French hens? One theory is that "French" was simply synonymous with "foreign," and this would make sense for our allegorical interpretation as well, for the theological virtues are not acquired from within but infused from without, given to us by God undeservedly.

Eggnog is a holiday favorite, although tonight let us honor this byproduct of the hen under its French name, *lait de poule.* We borrowed this recipe from *Le Journal des Femmes* and tweaked it, making it a little less sweet and a little more potent.

A French Connection is a simple and solid choice, but we are especially pleased with the Three French Hens cocktail. We asked our friend Andrew Anderson, chief mixologist at Balcones Distilling Company, to come up with a recipe that had Le Sirop de Monin for the "French" and egg white for the "hens," and he did not disappoint. Break out the bottle of Balcones Rumble that you bought for Ambrose's Day (see p. 25) and enjoy it in Andrew's utterly magical Three French Hens cocktail, publicized here for the first time.

THE FRENCH CONNECTION

1½ oz. cognac or brandy
¾ oz. amaretto

Build in an old-fashioned glass filled with ice.

LAIT DE POULE (FRENCH EGGNOG)

By Joel Brouzet

1 tbsp. sugar

1 egg yolk

3½ oz. milk

1 pinch of cinnamon

1 pinch of nutmeg

1½ oz. light rum (or bourbon, brandy, etc.)

In a saucepan, heat the milk. Be careful not to boil. In a separate bowl, mix the egg yolk and sugar for 4 to 5 minutes. Add the hot milk to the egg-sugar mixture, beating constantly with the whisk, until the mixture is homogeneous. Garnish with cinnamon and nutmeg.

THREE FRENCH HENS

By Andrew Anderson

1½ oz. Balcones Rumble

¾ oz. fresh lemon juice

½ oz. Monin blackberry syrup

1 egg white

Pour ingredients into a shaker filled with ice and shake forty times. Strain into a cocktail glass.

WINE AND BEER

Think poultry with your wine tonight. Australia's Purple Hen Wines, Texas' Lone Hen Winery, and Brengman Brothers' Runaway Hen label out of Michigan are a few examples. But perhaps the most appropriate is a French wine honoring a hen such as Château du Rouët's

Belle Poule or "Beautiful Hen" label. Belle Poule comes in red, rosé, and white, one for each of the French hens mentioned in the song.

As for beer, Old Speckled Hen is an English ale from the Morland Brewery that has been around since 1979. The brand has also been expanded to include Old Crafty Hen and Old Golden Hen. We will let you and your friends debate which hen represents which theological virtue.

LAST CALL

May the Holy Spirit infuse our hearts with faith, hope, and charity as quickly as this drink infuses our bloodstream.

DECEMBER 28—
"ON THE FOURTH DAY OF CHRISTMAS, MY TRUE LOVE GAVE TO ME FOUR CALLING BIRDS."

The earliest versions of this song have "colly birds" (blackbirds) instead of "calling birds." Although we're tempted to go with colly birds because of all the raven/blackbird connections, we are going to stick with calling birds because of its greater potential for Catholic symbolism. As calling birds, the four fowls represent the four Evangelists (Matthew, Mark, Luke, and John), calling out to the world the Good News of our salvation.

David and Karen Hickey made a delicious Four Cardinals cocktail to honor Princes of the Church Raymond Burke, Carlo Caffarra, Walter Brandmüller, and Joachim Meisner, all of whom called out for greater clarification on present Church teaching. The drink also works nicely, however, as a way of honoring the four Evangelists—cardinals are calling birds, right? The Omni Hotels, on the other hand, have a Four Calling Birds Cocktail. We suspect that the blackberries are a tie-in to colly birds, but the Crown Royal Black (a bolder version of Crown Royal) is a nice reminder of the four Evangelists proclaiming the reign of Christ the King (and it is okay to use frozen blackberries this time of year). We went a step further and topped ours off with soda water for extra pizzazz. If you can't find Crème de Mûre blackberry liqueur, look for Bols blackberry brandy, since blackberry liqueur and blackberry brandy are the same thing.

THE FOUR CARDINALS

By David and Karen Hickey
2 oz. bourbon
1½ oz. ruby red grapefruit
  juice

½ oz. Bärenjäger
½ oz. simple syrup
splash Fernet Branca

Pour all ingredients into a shaker filled with ice and shake forty times. Strain into a cocktail glass.

FOUR CALLING BIRDS

By Omni Hotels and Resorts
1½ oz. Crown Royal Black
1 oz. fresh lemon juice
¾ oz. Crème de Mûre blackberry liqueur (or Bols
  blackberry brandy)

¾ oz. maple syrup
soda water (optional)
3-6 blackberries

Muddle 3 blackberries in a highball glass. Add all liquid ingredients and stir until syrup is dissolved. Top with ice and garnish with remaining blackberries skewered on a cocktail stick.

WINE AND BEER

Okay, we tried to steer clear of colly birds, but we are five days shy of making or keeping any resolutions, so no judgments, please. You can honor the original phrasing of tonight's verse with something in honor of a blackbird. For wine, see if you can find a bottle produced by Blackbird Vineyards located in Napa Valley.

A beer from Seattle's Black Raven would be nice, such as the Grandfather Raven Imperial Stout, a big, boozy beer that hits the spot on a cold winter's night. Or maybe a Three-Eyed Raven from Brewery Ommegang, which has more of a national distribution.

And as for a calling bird, Shiner Ruby Redbird includes a "bold kick of ginger," a holiday spice that helps you find your call voice.

LAST CALL

May we always have the grace and strength to call out the faith like an apostle, with or without the help of liquid courage.

DECEMBER 29—
"ON THE FIFTH DAY OF CHRISTMAS, MY TRUE LOVE GAVE TO ME FIVE GOLDEN RINGS."

Why the sudden switch from birds to rings? Some historians think that the gold rings are a corruption of "goldspinks," a Scottish name for goldfinch, thereby making all of the gifts during the first seven days birds. But in our current version, the five golden rings can be seen as the Pentateuch or Torah, the first five books of the Old Testament (Genesis, Exodus, Numbers, Leviticus, and Deuteronomy). A ring is a sign of fidelity to a covenant (think weddings), and the Torah is all about fidelity to the Old Covenant that God made with Abraham.

Julie Cohn at A Cork, Fork, and Passport has outdone herself with her Rings of Gold cocktail recipe. If you have plenty of time to spare, are aiming high, and are seeking to impress whatever the cost, this visually stunning drink is the one to serve. Small bottles of edible gold flakes by Barnabas Blattgold, incidentally, can be purchased on amazon.com.

If you want something less complicated but are still hankering to eat gold (which is an end-of-year tradition—see p. 126), you can simply add a few flakes to your favorite glass of champagne. Let's call it a Sparkling Gold Ring. Or to make life even easier, turn to our wine suggestions for two already-made options.

Finally, we adapted a La Bomba cocktail from Magic Skillet to produce a *Drinking with Saint Nick* semi-original. The Gold Ringer is made from five ingredients (including gold tequila) and is garnished with a golden orange ring.

RINGS OF GOLD (SERVES 4)

By Julie Cohn

4 oz. Jack Daniel's Winter Jack Cider	2 oz. orange bitters
8 oz. apple cider	edible gold flakes with 1 oz. Winter Jack added

Add the Winter Jack, apple cider, and orange bitters to a cocktail shaker filled with ice and shake forty times. Strain into four cocktail glasses.

Open the bottle of edible gold flakes and pour in one ounce of Winter Jack. Reseal the bottle and shake: the more you shake, the smaller the gold flecks will become. Pour a little bit of the gold flecks into each glass. Each bottle of edible gold flakes is enough for four or five cocktails.

Place sugar ring on top of each glass (see below).

SPUN SUGAR GOLD RINGS

½ cup white sugar

Heat the sugar over medium high heat, stirring frequently. The sugar will start to clump together, then liquefy. Watch it very carefully at this stage: The moment it turns a light golden color, remove from the heat; otherwise you will overcook it and burn the sugar. Set aside to cool for a moment, then drizzle the sugar into rings on a foil or wax paper-lined baking sheet. Allow the sugar to harden, about five minutes, then place on top of the cocktail.

SPARKLING GOLD RING

white sparkling wine or   1 pinch of gold flakes
  champagne

Pour sparkling wine into a champagne coupe or flute glass. Crush gold flakes between your thumb and forefinger and sprinkle in.

GOLD RINGER

1½ oz. gold tequila   1 dash grenadine
¼ oz. Cointreau   sugar for rim
¼ oz. pineapple juice   1 orange wheel
¼ oz. orange juice

Rub the rim of the cocktail glass with wedge of orange. Dip it into superfine sugar. Pour all ingredients except grenadine in a shaker filled with ice and shake forty times. Strain into the cocktail glass and add grenadine for sunrise effect. Garnish with orange wheel (and stir before drinking).

Wine and Beer

A couple of wineries save you the trouble of tracking down gold flakes by adding it themselves to their sparkling wines. Look for Blue Nun 24k Gold Edition or a bottle of Jade Or de Malidain from the Loire Valley in France.

Wine maker Lot18 has also released a series of wines based on Lord of the Rings. Close enough.

For beer, (American) Golden Ale is another name for blonde ale, a moderately bitter and malty brew originally designed to transition mass market consumers to craft beers—not unlike God's promulgation of the Old Law to help mankind transition to the New Covenant. Examples include Goose Island Blonde Ale, Redhook Blonde, Sea Dog Windjammer Blonde, Catamount Gold, Hollywood Blonde, Pete's Wicked Summer Brew, Shiner Golden Ale, Big Wave Golden Ale, and Glütiny Golden Ale.

Belgian Golden Ales, on the other hand, have a light body and a surprising alcoholic kick (up to 9% ABV). Because Belgian Golden Ales are typically fermented three times (the last in the bottle), they have fine champagne-like carbonation and an imposing white head. One of the most famous brands is Duvel, brewed by Brouwerij Duvel Moortgat NV in Belgium. Although the name means "Devil," it can be baptized tonight for saintly use.

And one should never pass up an opportunity to drink Trappist beer, even if it is not a Golden Ale. The Brasserie d'Orval, the Belgian brewery within the Abbaye

Notre-Dame d'Orval, produces the spectacular and readily-available Belgian Pale Ale-style beer, Orval Trappist Ale. Orval is appropriate for the verse tonight given the fascinating story behind the logo and the monastery's name. "Matilde was a widow, and her wedding ring had accidentally fallen into the fountain. She prayed to the Lord and at once a trout rose to the surface with the precious ring in its mouth. Matilde exclaimed: 'Truly this place is a Val d'Or! [Valley of Gold].' In gratitude, she decided to establish a monastery on the site."

Finally, The Shmaltz Brewing Company in Clifton Park, New York has a Genesis Dry Hopped Sessional Ale to honor the first book of the Pentateuch, and SweetWater Brewing Company in Atlanta has an Exodus Porter to honor the second.

LAST CALL

May we value the wisdom of the five books of the Pentateuch more than five rings made of gold.

DECEMBER 30—
"ON THE SIXTH DAY OF CHRISTMAS, MY TRUE LOVE GAVE TO ME SIX GEESE A LAYING"

The laying of eggs is an obvious metaphor for new life, and so the six geese a laying are said to represent the six days of Creation (Gen. 1:3-31).

There are at least two liquors with an anserine name (that's a fancy term for gooselike, by the way; be sure to drop it casually into the conversation tonight with an insouciant air of intellectual superiority).

You can have Grey Goose in a *Drinking with Saint Nick* semi-original which is based on a variation of the Pink Lady called Six Geese a Laying: the Grey Goose (France's most famous vodka) for the geese, the egg white for their a layin', and the pineapple, lemon juice, apple brandy, cherry, and grenadine (make sure to get real grenadine made from real pomegranate) for the fruits of Creation.

Wild Geese Rare Irish Whiskey is a brand of reputable Irish whiskey, rum, and honey liqueur. Served neat with a splash of water, it is also a nice nod to the productive birds of the day.

SIX GEESE A LAYING COCKTAIL

1½ oz. Grey Goose vodka
1½ oz. apple brandy
½ oz. fresh lemon juice
½ oz. grenadine

1 egg white
1 Toschi amarena black
   cherry

Pour all ingredients into a shaker filled with ice and shake forty times. Strain into a cocktail glass.

BEER

We're not sure how many geese are on Goose Island, but a Goose Island beer is not a bad option for this evening.

DECEMBER 31—
"ON THE SEVENTH DAY OF CHRISTMAS, MY TRUE LOVE GAVE TO ME SEVEN SWANS A SWIMMING"

Seven swans a swimming can represent the seven gifts of the Holy Spirit, first mentioned in Isaiah 11:2-3: wisdom, understanding, counsel, fortitude, knowledge, piety, and fear of the Lord. And they also remind us of the seven Sacraments of the Church: Baptism, Confirmation, Holy Eucharist, Penance, Extreme Unction, Holy Orders, and Matrimony. In medieval bestiaries a swan was a symbol of Christ, for when the swan dives for fish, his body is never fully submerged, just as Christ's immersion in the tomb was only temporary. A Christ-like bird is fitting for today, since the seven gifts of the Holy Spirit were first listed in reference to the Messiah, and Jesus Christ is also the author of all seven Sacraments.

Kate and Drew Trgovac at A Bitter Spirit chose one of our favorite cocktail wines, Red Dubonnet, as the basis for their Seven Swans a-Swimming Cocktail on the grounds that swans are protected by the Queen of England and Her Majesty's favorite drink is Dubonnet. In a book that strains connections as much as it does cocktails, who are we to judge? It also makes sense to have a champagne drink for New Year's Eve; and the floating bubbles can remind us of our cygnine Lord, who was not submerged for long by death (and yes, "cygnine" is a hoity-toity way of saying "swan-like").

A simpler option is a White Swan cocktail which, between you and me, is virtually identical to a Disaronno and Milk (see p. 162).

SEVEN SWANS A-SWIMMING COCKTAIL

By Kate and Drew Trgovac

1 oz. Red Dubonnet   champagne, prosecco, or
1 tsp. Pernod   other sparkling wine
1 tsp. simple syrup

Combine the Dubonnet, Pernod, and simple syrup in a champagne flute. Top with champagne.

WHITE SWAN

1½ oz. amaretto liqueur   3 oz. milk

Build in an old-fashioned glass filled with ice and stir.

BEER

Thornbridge Brewery's Wild Swan Ale is a fine pale ale, but it is not available outside the United Kingdom. Real Ale Brewing Company in Blanco, Texas has a Sword Iron Swan Ale. Let the image of a sword recall the sevenfold gifts of the Spirit given in Confirmation that equip the soul to be a soldier of Christ. That said, the grace of the Holy Spirit may be easier to come by than a bottle of this ale, depending on where you live.

LAST CALL

May the gifts of the Holy Spirit and the Sacraments of the Church render us as graceful as a swan swimming gently upon still waters.

JANUARY 1—
"ON THE EIGHTH DAY OF CHRISTMAS, MY TRUE LOVE GAVE TO ME EIGHT MAIDS A MILKING"

Eight maids a milking call to mind the eight Beatitudes (Mt. 5.3-12). Like lowly milkmaids, the eight kinds of people whom Christ praises in the Beatitudes are humble or productive. To refresh your memory, those eight blessed souls are: the poor in spirit, mourners, the meek, those who hunger and thirst for justice, the merciful, the clean of heart, peacemakers, and those who are persecuted for justice's sake.

A Milk Punch is a fine choice for today: it is even listed as a "morning cocktail" and can thus be featured at a New Year's Day brunch as an alternative to a Bloody Mary. We include the standard version along with a delicious traditional Irish hot milk punch known as Scaitlin.

Disaronno and Milk is also a fitting tribute to busy milkmaids: The main ingredient, amaretto, was invented by a beautiful Italian innkeeper who posed for a Madonna painting by the Renaissance artist Bernardino Luini. Like the little drummer boy, the lovely maiden model showed her gratitude to Luini for this honor by doing what she did best, perfecting a liqueur made from almonds and apricots.

MILK PUNCH

½ tsp. sugar

2 oz. brandy (or 1 ½ oz. bourbon or other whiskey)

milk

nutmeg

Build alcohol and sugar in a highball glass filled with ice and top with milk. Stir gently. Sprinkle nutmeg on top.

SCAITLIN (IRISH HOT MILK PUNCH)

1 cup whole milk
¼ cup Irish whiskey
1 tbsp. honey

⅟₁₆ tsp. vanilla extract
nutmeg for garnish

Pour the milk and whiskey into a small saucepan and stir in the honey and vanilla. Heat slowly on low, not allowing the mixture to boil. Whisk to allow the honey and vanilla to dissolve and create a froth. Pour into a warm Irish coffee mug and sprinkle with nutmeg. Serve hot.

DISARONNO AND MILK

1½ oz. Disaronno amaretto
  liqueur

2 oz. milk

Build in an old-fashioned glass filled with ice and stir.

WINE AND BEER

Liebfraumilch is a semi-sweet white German wine that literally means "Our Dear Lady's milk" because it was first produced near the Church of Our Dear Lady in the city of Worms, Germany. Mary Our Dear Lady, however, would not mind sharing her wines with the milk maids today.

The Bruery in Orange County, California has a mostly-retired Twelve Beers of Christmas™ series, but their 8 Maids-a-Milking, a Belgian-style imperial milk stout, is still with us. If you cannot find any, there are a multitude of other milk stouts from which to choose.

LAST CALL

A toast: May the Spirit of the Beatitudes forever fill us with the milk of superhuman kindness.

January 2—
"On the Ninth Day of Christmas, My True Love Gave to Me Nine Ladies Dancing"

Nine ladies dancing can be seen as a metaphor for the nine choirs of angels. Even though as pure spirits angels are without sexual differentiation (or bodies that can dance for that matter), the image of dancing ladies is a fitting way to remember how the heavenly hosts must have rejoiced and danced with delight, so to speak, at the birth of their Creator.

In case you have forgotten, the nine orders or choirs of angels in ascending order are: Angels, Archangels, Principalities, Powers, Virtues, Dominations, Thrones, Cherubim, and Seraphim.

Joel Morehouse and Julia Tucker have invented a lovely drink which they have allowed us to dub Nine Ladies

Dancing. The beautiful color and champagne coupe glass are beguilingly feminine, while the gin and Pinot Grigio will have you cutting a rug in no time. The same goes for the entire bottle of scotch in Elana Lepkowski's Nine Ladies Dancing Punch, which can be prepared the day before a party.

NINE LADIES DANCING COCKTAIL

By Joel Morehouse and Julia Tucker
2 oz. gin
1 oz. Pinot Grigio
¾ oz. St. Germaine elder-
flower liqueur
¼ oz. Campari

Pour all ingredients into a mixing glass with ice and stir forty times. Strain into a champagne coupe or cocktail glass.

NINE LADIES DANCING PUNCH

By Elana Lepkowski
1 (750 ml) bottle blended scotch
2¼ cups Lustau East India solera sherry (or any high-quality cream sherry)
¾ cup fresh lemon juice
1½ cups vanilla cinnamon syrup (see below)
2 cups chai tea (made from 2 cups boiling water and 3 chai tea bags steeped for four minutes and allowed to cool)
2 tbsp. Angostura bitters
6 orange wheels, star anise, ice block (see note), for garnish

In a punch bowl or large container, combine scotch, sherry, lemon juice, syrup, tea, and bitters. Stir to combine. Refrigerate for 5 hours or overnight. When ready to serve, add an ice block and garnish as desired.

Note: To make an ice block, fill a Tupperware container ¾ full of water, adding rinsed cranberries if desired. Freeze overnight. To remove, let sit ten minutes at room temperature, then twist to remove, or run under hot water for five seconds.

VANILLA CINNAMON SYRUP

4 (3- or 4-inch) cinnamon sticks	1 cup sugar
1 vanilla bean, split and seeds scraped	1 cup water

In a medium saucepan, combine cinnamon sticks, vanilla bean seeds and pod, sugar, and water. Bring to a boil over medium high heat, remove from heat and let stand for one hour. Strain. The syrup can be refrigerated in an airtight container for up to two weeks.

BEER

Another of The Bruery's Twelve Beers of Christmas™ series that is not yet retired is their 9 Ladies Dancing, which the brewery bills as an imitation of tiramisu.

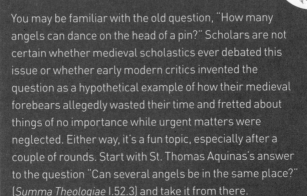

LAST CALL

You may be familiar with the old question, "How many angels can dance on the head of a pin?" Scholars are not certain whether medieval scholastics ever debated this issue or whether early modern critics invented the question as a hypothetical example of how their medieval forebears allegedly wasted their time and fretted about things of no importance while urgent matters were neglected. Either way, it's a fun topic, especially after a couple of rounds. Start with St. Thomas Aquinas's answer to the question "Can several angels be in the same place?" (*Summa Theologiae* I.52.3) and take it from there.

But if metaphysics isn't your thing—at least not during the Twelve Days of Christmas—cut to the chase and offer the following toast: May dancing ladies remind us of rejoicing angels, and may rejoicing angels help us praise our infant King.

JANUARY 3—
"ON THE TENTH DAY OF CHRISTMAS, MY TRUE LOVE GAVE TO ME TEN LORDS A LEAPING"

Ten lords a leaping may be seen as a representation of the Ten Commandments (Exodus 20:7-17; Deuteronomy 5:11-21). A lord worthy of the name not only lays down the law but also acts virtuously. Similarly, the Decalogue is not only a set of commandments but a map for becoming truly happy. As Moses told the people of Israel: "I call heaven and earth to witness this day, that I have set before you life and death, blessing and cursing. Choose therefore life, that both thou and thy seed may live" (Deuteronomy 30:19). Rules for a happy life? No wonder the lords are a leaping.

What also gets the lords leaping is a good fire in the hole. We asked our friend Andrew Anderson, chief mixologist at Balcones Distilling Company, to come up with a bold and virulent cocktail in honor of tonight's verse. Andrew responded with a recipe that includes: Balcones Brimstone, a one-of-a-kind whisky smoked with sunbaked Texas scrub oak; and Lapsang Souchong, a distinctive smoky dark tea from China produced by drying souchong leaves over an open fire of pinewood (the use of tea is a nice touch—very evocative of an English lord.) We tried regular black tea instead of Lapsang Souchong, and the cocktail still had an excellent smoky finish. And we think the drink is perfect as-is, but if you want it a little sweeter you can increase the amount of tea syrup to ½ ounce or more.

TEN LORDS A LEAPING

By Andrew Anderson

1½ oz. Balcones Brimstone
¼ oz. tea syrup (equal parts Lapsang Souchong tea and sugar, stirred until the sugar is dissolved)
3 dashes Angostura bitters
lemon twist for garnish

Build all liquid ingredients in an old-fashioned glass with ice and stir. Garnish with lemon.

BEER

2017 saw the production of The Bruery's latest installation of their Twelve Beers of Christmas™ series, their 10 Lords-a-Leaping, a dark imperial wit ale featuring 10 different spices. The Lost Abbey Brewery, on the other hand, has a potent Belgian Style Dark Farmhouse Ale called The Ten Commandments.

JANUARY 4—
"ON THE ELEVENTH DAY OF CHRISTMAS, MY TRUE LOVE GAVE TO ME ELEVEN PIPERS PIPING"

Eleven pipers piping recall the eleven faithful apostles: Peter (Simon Bar Jonah), Andrew, James the Great, John, Thomas, James the Less, Philip, Bartholomew or Nathaniel, Matthew, Simon the Zealot, and Jude or Thaddeus. Like the Pied Piper in the story, the apostles were able to attract a multitude of disciples or followers through the sweet melody of the Gospel. But unlike the Pied Piper, they didn't abscond with the town children, and they probably didn't wear "pied" (multicolored) clothing— that was more Joseph's style from the Book of Genesis.

Seagram's 100 Pipers Scotch and Duncan Piper's Pipers Can Blended Scotch Whisky both have the right name for the job tonight, and both are inexpensive, which suits a tribute to the humbly-born apostles. Put either scotch into a Blood and Sand cocktail and—voilà!—you have a *Drinking with Saint Nick* semi-original called Eleven Pipers Piping.

Piper Sonoma is the name of a California winery that makes a Brut sparkling wine. They couldn't resist the temptation to make their own 11 Pipers Piping champagne cocktail, and we couldn't resist the temptation to print it here.

ELEVEN PIPERS PIPING

¾–1 oz. Pipers scotch (100 Pipers or Pipers Can blended scotch)

1 oz. orange juice (blood orange if possible)

¾ oz. sweet vermouth

¾ oz. Cherry Heering liqueur

pipe-shaped orange twist for garnish

Pour all liquid ingredients into a shaker filled with ice and shake forty times. Strain into a cocktail glass. Using a vegetable peeler or paring knife, cut a section of orange rind about one and a half inches wide and three inches long and twist and curl into the shape of a pipe. Optional: flame the orange twist over the drink by holding it about two inches above a lit match for a few seconds (the goal is to caramelize the citrus oils without burning or sooting the peel). Rub the twist around the rim of the glass and then drop into the drink.

11 PIPERS PIPING (CHAMPAGNE COCKTAIL)

¾ oz. Cointreau
Piper Sonoma Brut sparkling wine

3 oz. cranberry juice

Chill all ingredients. Pour Cointreau and cranberry juice into a champagne flute and stir. Top with Piper Sonoma Brut.

WINE AND BEER

For the last several years The Bruery in Orange County, California has been producing seasonal brews for their Twelve Beers of Christmas™ series. This year, 2018, should be the year for an 11 Pipers Piping.

Going in a different direction, the Devil's Backbone Brewing Company in Virginia has a Five Apostles Saison "in homage to the five ecclesiastically named peaks in the region." Perhaps you can pour yourself two and one-fifth bottles to honor the eleven faithful apostles.

LAST CALL

A toast—To the pious pipers who followed our Lord: through their intercession, may we always answer the tune of Apostolic Tradition with a spring in our step and joy in our hearts.

JANUARY 5—
"ON THE TWELFTH DAY OF CHRISTMAS, MY TRUE LOVE GAVE TO ME TWELVE DRUMMERS DRUMMING"

Twelve drummers drumming can be seen as a symbol of the twelve articles of the Apostles' Creed. Think of it as marching to the beat of God's appointed drummers on the path to truth and salvation.

There are a couple of Twelve Drummers Drumming cocktail recipes floating around; but our favorite—which we happily include here—is a concoction made by the Hilton Hotels. But if twelve days of drinking are making it hard for you to keep pace with your companions, we offer you a shortcut. Take your favorite cocktail that requires a garnish, spear the garnish with a wooden cocktail stick, and—presto!—you have a "drumstick" that can transform any drink into a homage to tonight's verse. That's basically what we did with our Duodecimal Drummers-Be-Drummin' Old Fashioned—along with using Johnny Drum bourbon, which has lovely notes of caramel that complement any beat.

TWELVE DRUMMERS DRUMMING COCKTAIL

By Hilton Europe

1 oz. ruby port wine
½ oz. peach liqueur
1 oz. apple juice

1 tsp. Lagavulin scotch (or
   any smoky whisky)
peach and blackberry for
   garnish

Pour all liquid ingredients into a shaker filled with ice and shake forty times. Double strain (to remove ice shards) into an old-fashioned glass with ice and garnish with three small, thin peach slices and blackberry speared by a wooden cocktail stick.

DUODECIMAL DRUMMERS-BE-DRUMMIN' OLD FASHIONED

2 oz. Johnny Drum bourbon
1 tsp. simple syrup
dash of bitters, Angostura or
  orange

2 Luxardo or Toschi cherries,
  each impaled by a different
  cocktail stick to resemble a
  drumstick

Pour simple syrup, bourbon, and bitters in an old-fashioned glass. Stir and fill with ice. Garnish with the two "drumsticks."

WINE AND BEER

Bakkheia Wines in Australia has a Different Drummer label alluding to Henry David Thoreau's famous line, but the label works well as a tribute to the Apostolic Faith, which truly is different from all the others.

As for beer, look for The Bruery's next installment in its Twelve Beers of Christmas™ series—12 Drummers Drumming beer—in the year 2019.

EPIPHANY AND
THE TIME THEREAFTER
FROM JANUARY 6 TO FEBRUARY 2

For some, Epiphany closes out the observance of Christmas; for others, it merely kicks the season into a different gear. Both sides have a point, for Epiphany is not the celebration of the birth of the God-man, but it is the celebration of the God-man revealing Himself to all the nations. Why let the ember glow of Christmas warmth die out when you can fan it into a slightly different fire?

In this chapter, we offer something to wet your whistle while you pump the bellows.

EPIPHANY, JANUARY 6
(SUNDAY BETWEEN JANUARY 2 AND 8)

The great feast of the Epiphany, which is a holy day of obligation in most countries, celebrates the visit of the Magi to the newborn King in Bethlehem, and as such it celebrates the fact that Jesus Christ came to save not only the Jews but the Gentiles (represented by the Magi, Zoroastrian priestly scholars). The Magi are also called the Three Kings in accordance with two Old Testament prophecies that describe kings from Tharsis, Arabia, and Sheba bringing to the Messiah presents (Ps. 71:10) such as gold and frankincense (Is. 60:3-6).

The Epiphany drink, usually drunk on the vigil of the feast, is a wassail called Lamb's Wool (for more on wassails, see p. 108). The unusual name is probably due to the fuzzy appearance of the roasted apples, but it is also a nice tie-in to the Lamb of God who this day revealed Himself to all the nations. And there's even a nice little ditty to remind you of the instructions.

> With gentle Lambs wooll,
> Adde sugar, nutmeg, and ginger,
> With store of ale too,
> And thus ye must doe
> To make the Wassaile a swinger.

....

LAMB'S WOOL*

....

6 baking apples, cored   ¼ tsp. nutmeg

2 tbsp. to ½ cup brown sugar   ¼ tsp. cinnamon

2 qts. sweet cider or hard   ¼ tsp. ground ginger
   cider or ale—or a combi-
   nation of cider and ale

Peel and boil the apples, either whole or cut, until they are very soft and flaky. (A lengthier but more traditional alternative is to roast the apples in a baking pan at 450° F for an hour or until they are very soft and begin to burst.)

In a large saucepan, dissolve the sugar a few tablespoons at a time in cider or ale, tasting for sweetness. Add the spices. Bring to a boil and simmer for 10 to 15 minutes. Pour the liquid over the apples in a large punch bowl. Add nuts if desired or serve separately. Makes about eight one-cup servings.

For liqueurs, you can actually drink one of the Magi's presents: are you able to guess which one? Goldwasser is a strong root and herbal liqueur that includes flakes of suspended gold. (The gold, which hearkens back to the days of alchemy when gold was thought to have medicinal properties, is harmless.) Goldwasser is difficult to find in the U.S., but Goldschläger, a Swiss *cinnamon* schnapps, is easier to find and based on the same idea.

---

* From Evelyn Vitz's *A Continual Feast* (San Francisco: Ignatius Press, 1991), 167.

Or, have a semi-original cocktail based on the Tequila Old Fashioned that honors all three gifts: gold tequila for gold, bitters for myrrh ("myrrh" comes from the Aramaic word for bitter), and simple syrup for the sweet smell of frankincense. And when you drink a "Gifts of the Magi" you are also honoring Our Lord, since gold represents His kingship, myrrh His Passion, and frankincense His divinity. We used Jose Cuervo Especial Tequila Gold for our tests and were most pleased with the results. And, of course, the star anise represents that which led the wise men to the Savior.

A campy lowbrow backup is a Three Wise Men cocktail, a mixture of whiskies from Scotland, Tennessee, and Kentucky. After a couple of rounds of these, you will probably imitate the Wise Men and not make it back home by the same route.

Finally, there is an old cocktail recipe for a Star that we tinkered with by modifying the proportions and adding simple syrup, orange, and star anise—a reflection of the Magi's prudent versatility.

....

GIFTS OF THE MAGI

....

2 oz. gold tequila   1 lemon twist
½ tsp. simple syrup   1 star anise
2 dashes Angostura bitters

Pour all ingredients into an old-fashioned glass except star anise and stir. Add ice and crown with the star.

Three Wise Men

1 part Johnnie Walker
  scotch

1 part Jack Daniels whiskey
1 part Jim Beam whiskey

Add into a shot glass with equal parts.

Star

1½ oz. Calvados or apple
  brandy
1½ oz. gin
1 tbsp. grapefruit juice
1 tsp. simple syrup
  (optional)

1 dash dry vermouth
1 dash sweet vermouth
1 orange wheel with a star
  anise (optional)

Pour all liquid ingredients into a mixing glass with ice and stir
forty times. Strain into a cocktail glass and garnish with
orange wheel/star anise.

Beer and Wine

Lost Abbey in San Marcos, California has a Gift of the
Magi ale: "Gold in color and bittered with the bark of
Frankincense," they say of their product, "we have even
used the smallest amount of Myrrh which is an herb that
has roots in ancient winemaking as well."

Or, pull out your very best wine, since the Miracle at
Cana is traditionally believed to have occurred on the
same calendar day.

LAST CALL

In some parts of the world Epiphany is called "Little Christmas" because it is the final day for exchanging Christmas gifts. In the Irish counties of Cork and Kerry, it is also called "Women's Christmas." Irish men do all of the household chores today, while their womenfolk hold parties or go out with their friends, with pubs and restaurants holding special "Ladies' Night" attractions. Children also give special gifts to their mothers and grandmothers on this day. Use your imagination and apply these customs to your day.

FEAST OF THE HOLY FAMILY,
SUNDAY AFTER EPIPHANY
(SUNDAY AFTER CHRISTMAS)

This lovely feast pays tribute to the domestic life of Jesus, Mary, and Joseph. There are two legends about the Holy Family that provide inspiration for tonight's cocktail menu. According to a Sicilian superstition, a juniper bush courageously hid Jesus, Mary, and Joseph from Herod's soldiers, an act that God rewarded by bestowing on the plant the power of putting evil spirits to flight. Similarly, Mary washed the tiny garments of Jesus during their flight and spread them over the branches of a rosemary bush to dry them. In reward for this service to His Son, God conferred upon the rosemary, or "Mary's rose," a fragrant aroma.

These charming tales give us an idea for a Rosemary Martini. Gin, if you recall, is traditionally made from juniper berries.

ROSEMARY MARTINI

2 oz. gin   1 small sprig of rosemary
1 dash vermouth

Pour all ingredients except rosemary into a mixing glass with ice and stir forty times. Strain into a cocktail glass and garnish with rosemary. And if you don't have any rosemary on hand, use an olive, which will remind you of the olive orchards of Bethlehem.

BEER AND WINE

For beer, honor Our Lord with Salvator beer (p. 101) or St. Joseph with Spencer Trappist Ale, made by St. Joseph's Abbey in Spencer, Massachusetts.

For wine, honor the Blessed Virgin's tender motherhood with *Liebfraumilch*, a semi-sweet white German wine that literally means "Our Lady's milk." Château Tour St. Joseph is a winery in the Bordeaux region of France under the Haut-Médoc appellation that makes a number of wines, including a well-regarded Cru Bourgeois. The high-end winery Guigal in the Rhône region of France has a line of wines from its Saint-Joseph vineyard, which was once owned by the Jesuits. That area of the Rhône, which has 160 winemakers of various sizes, carries the AOC appellation Saint-Joseph (Delas Frères winery in the northern Rhône, for instance, makes a Saint-Joseph "Sainte-Epine"). Their mostly red wines are known for being hearty, leading one French connoisseur to make the pun that "Saint Joseph le charpentier" (carpenter) is now "Saint-Joseph charpenté" (robust).

Oh, what the heck: honor all three members of the Holy Family by throwing a party that includes all of the above.

LAST CALL

The traditional Collect for the feast also makes a fitting toast. "To our Lord Jesus Christ who, when He was subject to Mary and Joseph, sanctified domestic life with ineffable virtues. And may we all become partakers of the Holy Family's never-ending happiness as we learn from their example."

BAPTISM OF THE LORD JESUS CHRIST, JANUARY 13 (USUALLY, SUNDAY AFTER JANUARY 6)

Epiphany is about the manifestation (*epiphaneia*) of Christ to the Gentiles, and so to round out the celebration of this august feast the Church remembers one week later another divine manifestation, the Baptism of Jesus in the river Jordan by St. John the Baptist. It was on this occasion that Christ established Baptism as a Sacrament and was declared by a heavenly voice the Son of God in whom the Father is well pleased (Mt. 3:13-17).

On this day, celebrate Our Lord's baptism the way you would a Baptism or christening in your own family. Champagne and punch are traditional favorites for such a happy occasion. Or how about a champagne cocktail? (see Index for suggestions).

PLOUGH MONDAY, MONDAY AFTER EPIPHANY

In some parts of England, the Monday after the Twelve Days of Christmas is traditionally known as Plough Monday, the time to say goodbye to Christmas merriment and return to the grindstone—or plow or desk or whatever. Noteworthy customs for today include blackening one's face to disguise one's identity, dragging around a decorated plough, and shouting "Penny for the ploughboys!" There is also molly dancing, a form of English Morris dance that involves a troupe of male dancers, one of whom—the "molly" or milquetoast—is attired as a woman. For some, cross-dressing on Twelfth Night just isn't enough.

An easier and less controversial option is to have a drink. We don't know any "ploughmen," but we do know plenty of people who could use a stiff one to ease their transition back to the daily grind. In honor of this tradition, turn to your favorite English beer or ale (Newcastle, Speckled Hen, etc.). Or for something warm on a cold work night, play on the theme of the day with a Snow Plow:

SNOW PLOW

1 oz. Bailey's Irish cream
1 oz. coconut rum
½ oz. creme de cacao
cocoa sprinkles

10 oz. hot chocolate, or
   different amount if your
   glass is smaller
whipped cream

Pour Bailey's, rum, creme de cacao, and hot chocolate into a mug or Irish coffee cup and stir. Top with whipped cream and sprinkle a little cocoa onto it.

LAST CALL

A toast: May the joys and blessings of the Christmas season forever soften our toils at the plow.

CANDLEMAS: PURIFICATION OF THE BLESSED VIRGIN MARY (PRESENTATION OF THE LORD), FEBRUARY 2

When does the Christmas season end? Vigorous debate swirls around this seemingly simple question. In the post-Vatican-II calendar, the Christmas season formally ends on the Feast of the Baptism of Jesus, which in the U.S. falls either on the first Sunday after January 6 or the following Monday. The Christmas season in the Novus Ordo or "Ordinary Form" of the Roman Rite thus has seventeen days more or less.

In the traditional calendar, some people say that it ends after the liturgical season called "Time after Epiphany," the length of which varies depending on the date of Easter. The later Easter comes, the longer is the season of Epiphany and, by extension, the longer is Christmastide. Since the Time after Epiphany (which was replaced by "Ordinary Time" in the post-Vatican II calendar) can have as many as six Sundays—and the season of pre-Lent or Septuagesima doesn't begin until the following Sunday—you can have more than fifty days of the Christmas season according to this form of counting.

Still others claim that the Christmas season is a forty-day block, beginning on December 25 and ending today on February 2. Hence the poem that commands Christmas revelers to put away their holiday decorations on the evening of February 1:

> Down with the rosemary, and so
> Down with the bays and mistletoe;
> Down with the holly, ivy, all,
> Wherewith ye dress'd the Christmas Hall.
>> —Robert Herrick (1591–1674), "Ceremony
>> upon Candlemas Eve"

Since we personally tend to stretch out our festivities as long as possible, we're voting for the "Time after Epiphany" interpretation when this season is long and the "February 2" interpretation when it is short.

Either way, today's feast is a big deal. Forty days after giving birth to Our Lord and in keeping with the Mosaic

Law, Our Lady presented Jesus in the Temple and was ritually purified (Lk. 2:22-32). Subsequently, on February 2, the traditional Roman calendar keeps the Feast of the Purification of the Blessed Virgin Mary and the new Roman calendar (post-Vatican II) keeps the Feast of the Presentation of the Lord. The traditional feast is also nicknamed "Candlemas" (Mass of the Candles) because it was the occasion for great candlelight processions to chase away the darkness of winter and to celebrate Jesus Christ Who, as the prophet Simeon puts it on this day, is a "Light for the revelation of the Gentiles." Candles would be blessed on this day and used in the home throughout the year.

A nice way to commemorate the grand Candlemas processions of old is with a flaming, minty after-dinner drink called a Medieval Candle. The wide mouth of a cocktail or liqueur glass works best; we found that a snifter, with its narrow top, does not properly combust the surface fumes. (It also helps that the ingredients are at least at room temperature.) Finally, the 100-proof Southern Comfort is preferable for combustion purposes. And don't worry: some of that alcohol will be burned off.

MEDIEVAL CANDLE

½ oz. white crème de menthe

½ oz. Southern Comfort (100 proof if available)

Build ingredients in a small cocktail glass or liqueur glass and light the top.

Turn off the lights in order to enjoy the full effect. It will be tempting to let the mesmerizing blue flame continue burning, but remember that the longer it does, the hotter it will make the rim of the glass (and we do mean hot). You may even need to pour the drink into another glass to be on the safe side. And yes, you'll want to blow out the flame before attempting to consume.

Another option, and perhaps a safer one at that, is dipping back into the Second Day of Christmas and having a delicious Turtle Dove Martini or Chocolate Turtle Martini (see p. 145). Both drinks pay tribute to the offering that Joseph and Mary made at the Temple on this day (see Lk. 2:23-24).

LAST CALL

One of the old candle blessings for this day makes an ideal toast. "To our good Lord, a Light to the revelation of the Gentiles, who was presented in the Temple on this day. May we one day be presented in the Holy Temple of His glory, inflamed by the fire of His most sweet charity." And thanks be to God for a long and lustrous, merry and memorable, Christmas season.

Acknowledgments

L ike a great Christmas banquet, this book is the result of many hands working together. During the Advent and Christmas season of 2017-2018, I needed help coming up with drink ideas for the different feasts, O antiphons, and verses of "The Twelve Days of Christmas," and so I turned to the Facebook followers of *Drinking with the Saints*. Their willingness to help and their wise counsel were extraordinary. I tried to keep track of all the contributors and their contributions as best as I could in the following list: forgive me if I left anyone out.

The preface at the beginning of this book is a modified version of "How to Drink Like a Saint," an article originally printed in the May 12, 2015 edition of Crisis magazine. It is reprinted with permission.

Andrew Anderson of Balcones Distilling Company for inventing cocktails for the Feast of St. Ambrose and for the verses for the Third and Tenth days of Christmas;

Michael Astfalk for his suggestions regarding the First, Fourth, Fifth, and Ninth Days of Christmas;

Randy Aust for his suggestion regarding the December 18 O Antiphon;

Stephen Barnes for his suggestions regarding the Feast of Saint Spiridion;

Michelle Barrett for her suggestions regarding the December 21 and 23 O Antiphons and for the verse "On the First Day of Christmas";

Tanner Dimmick for sharing the recipe to his Golden Hour cocktail;

Ray Felderhoff for his suggestions regarding the feasts of Saint Spiridion and Saint Dominic of Silos; for the December 18, 19, 21, 22, and 23 O Antiphons; and for the verses on the First, Fourth, Fifth, and Sixth Days of Christmas;

Karen Hickey for her suggestion regarding the December 18 O Antiphon and for her cocktail "The Four Cardinals" which we used for the verse "On the Fourth Day of Christmas";

John Kalitka for his suggestions regarding the feasts of Blessed Franco Grotti, Saint Spiridion, and Saint Nino; for the December 17, 20, 21, 22, and 23 O Antiphons; for Twelfth Night; and for the verses on the Fifth, Seventh, Ninth, and Eleventh Days of Christmas;

Rob Kirby for his suggestions regarding the December 19 and 20 O Antiphons and for the verse "On the Fifth Day of Christmas";

Paul Krog for his suggestions regarding the feasts of Saint Francis Xavier, Blessed Franco Grotti, Saint Spiridion, Blessed Urban V, and Saint Thomas the Apostle; and for the December 17, 19, 20, 21, and 22 O Antiphons;

Michael Krom for his suggestions regarding the feast of St. Nicholas;

Peter Kwasniewski for sharing two of his cocktail inventions for the feast of St. Nicholas;

Sue Mach for her suggestions regarding the December 17 O Antiphon;

Mary Machado for her suggestions regarding the feast of Saint Sabbas; for the December 18, 19, 20, 21, 22, and 23 O Antiphons; and for the verses on the First, Fifth, and Sixth Days of Christmas;

Joel Morehouse and Julia Tucker for their Nine Ladies Dancing Cocktail;

Kathy Williams for her suggestion regarding the December 17 O Antiphon;

The amazing team at Regnery Publishing for their hard work and support;

Most of all, I wish to thank my faithful turtle dove and favorite *compotrix* Alexandra Foley for her unflagging support of the writing—and the lab work.

WORKS CONSULTED

Alexander, Patrick and Kaplan, Mitchell. *The Booklovers' Guide to Wine: A Celebration of the History, the Mysteries and the Literary Pleasures of Drinking Wine.* Mango, 2017.

Amis, Kingsley. *Everyday Drinking.* New York, Bloomsbury, 2008.

Augustine. *Confessions.* 2nd ed. Translated by F. J. Sheed. Indianapolis: Hackett, 2006.

Blume, Lesley M.M. *Let's Bring Back: The Cocktail Edition.* San Francisco: Chronicle Books, 2012.

Breviarum Romanum. 4 vols. Ratisbona, 1939.

Butler's Lives of the Fathers, Martyrs, and Other Saints. Edited by F. C. Husenbeth. 4 vols. Great Falls, MT: St. Bonaventure Publications, 1997.

Carosso, Vincent P. *The California Wine Industry, 1830-1895.* Berkeley: University of California Press, 1951.

Catholic Encyclopedia. 25 vols. New York: The Gilmary Society, 1907-1912. Available online at http://www.newadvent.org/cathen/.

Chow.com

CocktailDB: The Internet Cocktail Database. http://www.cocktaildb.com/index. Retrieved June 2013-June 2014.

Cohn, Julie. *A Cork, Fork, and Passport,* https://acorkfork andpassport.com/rings-of-gold-cocktail/. Retrieved January 2018.

Daiches, David. *Scotch Whiskey: Its Past and Present.* Edinburgh: Birlinn Ltd., 1995.

Doeser, Linda. *The Cocktail Bible.* Bath: Parragon, 2004.

Foley, Michael P. *Drinking with the Saints: The Sinner's Guide to a Holy Happy Hour.* Washington, D.C.: Regnery Publishing, 2015.

Why Do Catholics Eat Fish on Friday? The Catholic Origin to Just About Everything. New York: Palgrave Macmillan, 2005.

Gordon, Harry Jerrold. *Gordon's Cocktail & Food Recipes*. New York: Bloomsbury, 1934.

Graham, Colleen. About.com: Cocktails. http://cocktails.about.com/. Retrieved January 2018.

Grant, Leigh. *Twelve Days of Christmas: A Celebration and History*. New York: Harry N. Abrams, 1995.

Guéranger, Prosper. *The Liturgical Year*. Translated by Laurence Shepherd. 15 vols. Great Falls, MT: St. Bonaventure Publications, 2000.

Hartigan, Julie. *KDHamptons: The Luxury Lifestyle Diary of the Hamptons,* http://www.kdhamptons.com/. Retrieved December 2017.

Heimermann, Marc. SantoVino.com, now defunct.

Henriques, E. Frank. *The Signet Encyclopedia of Whiskey, Brandy & All Other Spirits*. New York: Signet Library, 1979.

Holy Bible, The. Douay-Rheims translation. Baltimore: John Murphy Co., 1914.

Lefebvre, Gaspar. *Saint Andrew Daily Missal*. St. Paul, MN: E. M. Lohmann Co., 1952.

Lichine, Alexis. *Alexis Lichine's New Encyclopedia of Wines & Spirits*. New York: Alfred A. Knopf, 1985.

Marinacci, Barbara and Rudy. *California's Spanish Place-Names: What They Mean and How They Got There*. Houston, TX: Gulf Publishing Co., 1997.

McGuire, E.B. *Irish Whiskey: A History of Distilling, the Spirit Trade, and Excise Controls in Ireland*. New York: Barnes and Noble, 1973.

Orvall Brewery website. http://www.orval.be/en/8/Brewery. Retrieved January 2018.

Oxford English Dictionary. 2nd ed. Available online at http://dictionary.oed.com/.

Powell, Fred. *The Bartender's Standard Manual*. New York: Wings Books, 1971.

Rituale Romanum. Rome: Desclee, 1943.

Robinson, Jancis. *The Oxford Companion to Wine,* 2nd ed. Oxford: Oxford University Press, 1999.

The Roman Martyrology, ed. J. B. O'Connell. Westminster, MD: The Newman Press, 1962.

Sutcliffe, Serena. *André Simon's Wineries of the World,* 2nd ed. New York: McGraw-Hill, 1981.

Tarling, W.J. *Café Royal Cocktail Book*. London: Pall Mall, 1937.

Aquinas, Thomas. *Summa Theologiae.*

Trapp, Maria von. *Around the Year with the Trapp Family.* New York: Pantheon, 1955.

Trgovac, Drew and Kate. *A Bitter Spirit,* http://www.abitterspirit.com/. Retrieved December 2017.

United Kingdom Bartender's Guild. *Approved Cocktails.* London: Pall Mall, 1937.

Vitz, Evelyn Birge. *A Continual Feast: A Cookbook to Celebrate the Joys of Family and Faith Throughout the Christian Year.* San Francisco Ignatius Press, 1985.

Weiser, Francis X. *Handbook of Christian Feasts and Customs: The Year of the Lord in Liturgy and Folklore.* New York: Harcourt, Brace and World, 1958.

Whitaker, Julie and Whitelaw, Ian. *A Pocket Guide to Cocktails.* Bath: Parragon, 2013.

Winslow, Joyce. *Mr. Boston Bartender's Guide: 50th Anniversary Edition.* New York: Warner Books, 1984.

Younger, William. *Gods, Men, and Wine.* London: The Wine and Food Society, 1966.

Zmirak, John and Matychowiak, Denise. *The Bad Catholic's Guide to Good Living.* New York: Crossroad, 2005.

The Bad Catholic's Guide to Wine, Whiskey, and Song. New York: Crossroad, 2007.

INDEX OF HOLY DAYS AND OTHER EVENTS

Index of Beverages

Italicized entries indicate drinks that are original to *Drinking with the Saints* or *Drinking with Saint Nick*.